President John F. Kennedy

In His Own Words

"*HIS GREATEST accomplishment was that he gave us the strength to believe we were better than we had thought.*"

RICHARD N. GOODWIN

Secretary General, International Peace Corps Secretariat

RELIGIOUS VIEWS OF

President John F. Kennedy

In His Own Words

COMPILED BY

Rev. Nicholas A. Schneider

B. HERDER BOOK CO.

St. Louis—London

1965

To Jacqueline Kennedy

INTRODUCTION

★

THE PUBLIC PAPERS OF PRESIDENT JOHN F. KENNEDY *comprise three volumes containing 2,632 double-column quarto pages. Among the 1,557 items of varying lengths are formal addresses, remarks, exchanges of greetings, memorandums, letters, news conferences, interviews, statements, telegrams, special messages, joint statements, toasts, reports, and proclamations. From them we learn the many roles the President plays—administrator, mediator, head of State, creator of national policy, interpreter of American principles. Above all, they show us the President in his foremost role: leader of the American people.*

President Kennedy assumed each of these roles with enthusiasm, vigor, and zeal. To them he brought a deep sense of history and a profound understanding of the United States' position of responsibility and leadership in the world of the twentieth century. Much of his work dealt directly with the business of government: proposals for legislation, reports on government activities, recommendations for further action. In dealing with the bureaus of government, his thoughts and words were businesslike in tone.

But in the other functions of his public service, he was a man of letters. His formal addresses, remarks, statements and proclamations mark him as one gifted in the use of the English language. American literature has been enriched by his contributions. With his tragic assassination, our nation suffered the loss not only of a dynamic young leader, but also of a man who was exceptionally articulate as American Presidents go.

Among his papers can be found a number of statements of a religious character, small by comparison with his total output, but broad enough to give us an idea of his religious views. He was not constantly quoting the Bible. Quotations from political leaders were much more frequent, Thomas Jefferson being his favorite. He very seldom referred to the fact that he was a Catholic, not because he wished us to ignore it, but because he was the President of the United States and took it for granted that his Catholic principles committed him to carry out the responsibilities of his office as perfectly and completely as he could. But his references to religion do reveal to us a man having a firm faith in God and his country, a deep trust in Divine Providence and the future of mankind, and a sincere love for all men which expressed itself in a willingness to involve himself with their problems anywhere on the globe.

This collection of the religious thought of President Kennedy is divided into five sections: Remarks and Addresses, Proclamations and Communiques, Answers to Questions proposed at News Conferences, Excerpts, and an Appendix containing some proclamations not found in the Public Papers. The presentation of material in each section is chronological.

Most of the items were addressed to audiences gathered for religious purposes or representing religious groups, or to commemorate religious observations. Some were spoken at places of religion, such as his talk at the Mormon Temple in Salt Lake City. Perhaps the best item in this collection is his speech before the Protestant Council of the City of New York, not because it contains the most references to God, for it does not, but because his thoughts on the Family of Man give us his whole basic outlook on how the Christian man, if he is to be true to his principles, must concern himself vitally with the needs of his fellow man.

Edward Schillebeeckx, O.P., a Catholic theologian, recently wrote: "In the past, a dualistic anthropological conception misled Christians into considering grace and redemption as a matter for God and the soul of man to deal with, so much so that the whole *range of earthly life and of human responsibility for the terrestrial future of mankind seemed to be relegated to the fringe of Christianity; one ran the risk of disregarding the truly Christian values of building the world and of promoting the advancement of peoples, thereby relinquishing the chore to those who called themselves non-Christians."* (The Church and Mankind, *p. 86. Paulist Press/Glen Rock, N.J. 1965.*)

President Kennedy was not so misled. He saw the "truly Christian values of building the world and of promoting the advancement of peoples," and brought the full power of the Presidency to bear in working for those goals. That is why he stands as an exemplar of the genuine American and genuine Christian in the twentieth century.

Nearly all of the items presented here, together with their titles and explanatory notes, are taken from the Public Papers of the Presidents, John F. Kennedy, 1961, 1962, 1963, *published in three volumes by the United States Government Printing Office. A few are not found there, but in the* Federal Register, *volumes 26, 27, and 28. These are added by way of Appendix.*

It is the editor's hope that this collection will contribute to a fuller understanding and greater appreciation of President John F. Kennedy.

NICHOLAS A. SCHNEIDER

CONTENTS

★

2. PROCLAMATIONS AND COMMUNIQUES

APPENDIX

I

REMARKS AND ADDRESSES

REMARKS ON GREETING REPRESENTATIVES OF THE
BAPTIST WORLD ALLIANCE AT THE WHITE HOUSE
FEBRUARY 2, 1961

I want to express my great appreciation for you coming here today and I am most impressed in hearing the litany of places—Japan, Korea, the Congo.

It is a wonderful thing, what you are doing. Some of you will be away for 5 years. You have a great tradition in your denomination of freedom and you can't have religious freedom without political freedom. The people of this country are strongly behind you and any help that we can give should be made known.

As I said in the State of the Union Message—one of the great ironies is that the Communists have been able to secure great devotion to their program and too often our people are identified with a devotion to material things. You are helping to change this.

★

REMARKS AT THE DEDICATION BREAKFAST OF
INTERNATIONAL CHRISTIAN LEADERSHIP, INC.
FEBRUARY 9, 1961

Mr. Chairman, Dr. Graham, Mr. Vice President— gentlemen:

I think it is most appropriate that we should be

gathered together for this morning's meeting. This country was founded by men and women who were dedicated or came to be dedicated to two propositions: first, a strong religious conviction, and secondly a recognition that this conviction could flourish only under a system of freedom.

I think it is appropriate that we pay tribute to this great constitutional principle which is enshrined in the First Amendment of the Constitution: the principle of religious independence, of religious liberty, of religious freedom. But I think it is also important that we pay tribute and acknowledge another great principle, and that is the principle of religious conviction. Religious freedom has no significance unless it is accompanied by conviction. And therefore the Puritans and the Pilgrims of my own section of New England, the Quakers of Pennsylvania, the Catholics of Maryland, the Presbyterians of North Carolina, the Methodists and the Baptists who came later, all shared these two great traditions which, like silver threads, have run through the warp and the woof of American history.

No man who enters upon the office to which I have succeeded can fail to recognize how every President of the United States has placed special reliance upon his faith in God. Every President has taken comfort and courage when told, as we are told today, that the Lord "will be with thee. He will not fail thee nor forsake thee. Fear not—neither be thou dismayed."

While they came from a wide variety of religious backgrounds and held a wide variety of religious beliefs, each of our Presidents in his own way has placed a special trust in God. Those who were strongest intellectually were also strongest spiritually.

Today our Nation is passing through another time of trial. In many ways, our dangers and our problems are far greater—and certainly infinitely more complex. We will need to draw upon the best that this Nation has—often—and draw upon it physically and intellectually and materially.

But we need also to call upon our great reservoir of spiritual resources. We must recognize that human collaboration is not enough, that in times such as these we must reach beyond ourselves if we are to seek ultimate courage and infinite wisdom.

It is an ironic fact that in this nuclear age, when the horizon of human knowledge and human experience has passed far beyond any that any age has ever known, that we turn back at this time to the oldest source of wisdom and strength, to the words of the prophets and the saints, who tell us that faith is more powerful than doubt, that hope is more potent that despair, and that only through the love that is sometimes called charity can we conquer those forces within ourselves and throughout all the world that threaten the very existence of mankind.

Keeping in mind that "when a man's ways please the Lord, he maketh even his enemies to be at peace with him," let us go forth to lead this land that we love, joining in the prayer of General George Washington in 1783, "that God would have you in His holy protection, that He would incline the hearts of the citizens . . . to entertain a brotherly love and affection for one another . . . and finally that He would most graciously be pleased to dispose us all to do justice, to love mercy, and to demean ourselves with . . . the characteristics of the Divine Author of our blessed religion, without an humble imitation of whose example we can never hope to be a happy nation."

The guiding principle and prayer of this Nation has been, is now, and shall ever be "In God We Trust."

Thank you.

[*The President spoke first to the gentlemen in the hotel's main ballroom, and then to the ladies in the east room.*]

Madam Chairwoman, Dr. Graham, Mr. Vice President,

It seems to me that in the true Christian spirit next year we should all sit down together, and that we should have gentlemen and ladies pray and reason together, and not confine them in different rooms.

But we are glad we came here—the Vice President and I came under the protection of Dr. Graham.

I do want to say that it is a pleasure to be here and to have participated in the breakfast this morning. I had an opportunity in the White House the other day to talk to a group of men and women from the Baptist World Alliance who have been missionaries, some in the Congo, one lady who has been in Bengal, India, since 1926, others who have been in Thailand and Korea.

I do not regard religion as a weapon in the cold war. I regard it as the essence of the differences which separate those on the other side of the Iron Curtain and ourselves.

The whole basis of the struggle is involved in the meeting this morning: our strong belief in religious freedom, our strong conviction, as I attempted to say in my inaugural, that the blessings which come to us come not from the generosity of the state but from the hand of God—and this alternate concept that the state is the master and the people the servants.

This is really the essence of the issue. We cannot have religious freedom without political freedom, and therefore what we really need is not to confuse a system of freedom with one of disinterest, unin-

6

terest, cynicism, materialism, but like the ladies and gentlemen I talked to the other day, who have been willing to spend their lives under the most difficult of circumstances, in great hardships, in order to to carry the message in which they have a great conviction, it seems to me it shows a lesson for us all.

We must match that faith. We must demonstrate in our lives, whatever our responsibility may be, that we care deeply.

I see no reason why the servants of the Communist system should be marked by a discipline and strong conviction in the ultimate success of their cause. I believe that our cause is just, that ultimately it will be successful. But it can only be successful if we demonstrate our strong conviction in it.

Religious freedom and religious conviction are the two hallmarks of American society, and therefore as a strong believer in both, I wanted to say that I deem it an honor to share this evidence of our common belief in these two great principles at this breakfast this morning. What we do this morning, I hope we can do every day.

Thank you.

[*The ninth annual prayer breakfast sponsored by the International Christian Leadership, Inc., a nondenominational group of laymen, was held at the Mayflower Hotel in Washington. William C. Jones of Los Angeles, Calif., a leader in the group, served as host. Frank Carlson, U.S. Senator from Kansas, and Mrs. Olin D. Johnston, wife of U.S. Senator Johnston of South Carolina, acted as chairmen. The evangelist, Dr. Billy Graham, led in prayer.*]

I want to express my great satisfaction in welcoming you to the White House again, and to tell you how grateful I am for your generosity. These Torahs I know have special significance for you, and particularly this one, which is so intimately associated with the founder here in the United States, one which is brought from Europe and which has been part of your life. So that I am doubly appreciative to you for being willing to part with it and present it to us here today.

I think, as the Rabbi said, that the significance of this ceremony is not merely a gift of an ancient document, but that in a very real sense the great issue today is between, as he said, the supremacy of the moral law which is initiated, originated, and developed in the Bible, and which has special application here today.

I've never felt that we should attempt to use the great impulse towards God and towards religion, which all people feel, as an element in a cold war struggle. Rather, it's not an arm, it is the essence of the issue—not the organization of economy so much, but as the supremacy of moral law, and therefore the right of the individual, his rights to be protected by the state and not be at the mercy of the state.

In the Inaugural Address, which the Rabbi mentioned, I said that the basic issue was that the rights the citizen enjoyed did not come from the state but rather came from the hand of God. And it's written here (pointing to the Torah). And it is written in the Old and New Testaments.

So I'm grateful to you, and I want you to know that in coming here today I think it symbolizes the happy relations which exist between all religious groups, and must continue to exist in this country if we are to be worthy of our heritage.

So, Rabbi, I'm grateful to you. There is no gift which could please me more—and I'm delighted to welcome you to our house.

[*The President spoke in the Rose Garden at the White House, following the presentation of a Sacred Torah by Rabbi Maurice N. Eisendrath, president of the Union of American Hebrew Congregations, and Emil N. Paar, chairman of its board of trustees. The Torah was brought to the United States from Bohemia in 1846 by Rabbi Isaac Mayer Wise, founder of American Reform Judaism. Dating from the 18th century, the scroll had been in the ark of the Isaac M. Wise Temple in Cincinnati.*]

★

REMARKS TO THE OFFICERS OF THE NATIONAL CONFERENCE OF CHRISTIANS AND JEWS
NOVEMBER 21, 1961

Gentlemen:

I want to express my great pleasure at having you here today at the White House. I think your efforts in this field represent a very valuable service to our country. It has always seemed to me that when we all—regardless of our particular religious convictions—draw our guidance and inspiration, and really in a sense moral direction from the same general area, the Bible, the Old and the New Testaments, we have every reason to believe that our various religious denominations should live together in the closest harmony.

We have a great advantage, really, in so much of the world, in having such common roots, and therefore though our convictions may take us in different directions in our faith, nevertheless the basic presumption of the moral law, the existence of God, man's relation to Him—there is generally consensus on those questions.

So that we should set a happy model for the world, but like all things, these things cannot be taken for granted. Your efforts, really, over the last period of 30 years, I think have done perhaps more than any other factor in our national life to provide for harmonious living among our different religious groups.

I think there are still important tasks ahead, so I am delighted to hear, Doctor, that your group is committing itself to an intelligent and nonpartisan and open discussion—continued discussion, really —of the relationships between the state and religion.

It, after all, was a matter which occupied our Founding Fathers, and should occupy our attention; and I am hopeful that the fact that you are discussing it will be another evidence of what an open and happy society we live in. So I welcome you here. I congratulate you for the efforts you are making in this area. You are performing a valuable function as citizens. And therefore, speaking as President, and personally, we want to emphasize how much your work is appreciated, how valuable it is, and what a service you're rendering.

Thank you.

[*The President spoke in the Rose Garden at the White House. During his remarks he referred to Dr. Lewis Webster Jones, president of the National Conference of Christians and Jews.*]

Senator, Judge, Mr. Speaker, Mr. Justice, Governor, gentlemen:

I want to, as President, express my appreciation to all those whose efforts make this breakfast possible. This is only one of a worldwide effort, I believe, to build a closer and more intimate association among those of different faiths in different countries and in different continents, who are united by a common belief in God, and therefore united in a common commitment to the moral order—and as Governor Daniels said, the relationship of the individual to the state.

The effort made in New Delhi among the World Council of Churches, the efforts that have been made in Europe to build better understanding among men and women of different faiths, the effort made in this country, I believe are most important and most essential.

I do not suggest that religion is an instrument of the cold war. Rather it is the basis of the issue which separates us from those who make themselves our adversary. And at the heart of the matter, of course, is the position of the individual—his importance, his sanctity, his relationship to his fellow men, his relationship to his country and his state. This is in essence the struggle, and it is necessary, therefore, that in these difficult days, when men and women who have strong religious convictions are beleaguered by those who are neither hot nor cold, or by those who are icy cold, it is most important that we make these common efforts—as we do this morning. So I congratulate you all, and express appreciation to you and hope that it will serve as an inspiration to others in other parts of our country.

I believe yesterday we saw an interesting contrast in the response which Colonel Glenn made as to whether he had prayed, and he said that he had not, that he had made his peace with his Maker many years before, and the statement made by Titov in which during his flight, as he flew over the Soviet Union he realized, he said, the wonders of the Communist system.

I preferred Colonel Glenn's answer because I thought it was solidly based, in his own life, in his activities in his church, and I think it reflects a quality which we like to believe and I think we can believe is much a part of our American heritage. So I congratulate you.

In our program this morning there is a quotation from Lincoln which I think is particularly applicable today. He said, "I believe there is a God. I see the storm coming and I believe He has a hand in it. If He has a part and place for me, I believe that I am ready."

We see the storm coming, and we believe He has a hand in it, and if He has a place and a part for us, I believe that we are ready.

[*The President spoke first to the gentlemen in the hotel's main ballroom and then to the ladies in the state and east rooms.*]

Ladies,

Last year I expressed some concern that instead of having been separated at these breakfasts—the pharisees and the publicans and the sinners and the saints—that the separation occurred on the basis of sex and not on those who should have been in the front room and those who were in the back room.

I do want to say, however—express my appreciation to you for the effort that you are making, to tell you how valuable I think it is that in this Capital of this most important country, upon which so much depends, that these breakfasts should be held, and that this demonstration of our commitment should be made.

We bear great responsibilities and great burdens not only to ourselves in this country but to so many around the world whose future hangs in the balance and depends so much on us.

We may not feel that our efforts are always appreciated, and I am not sure that that is so important, but we want to make sure that our efforts are effective, and that this generation—which faces the greatest challenges that any country, any free people, have ever faced, and moves in the midst of the greatest of opportunities and the greatest of dangers—that we shall meet our responsibility, which carries with it an obligation to our country, but I think in a larger sense carries with it an obligation to all those who desire to live a life of freedom and a life which permits them to participate with their neighbors and with God in the way they choose.

So I commend you for the example you set to us all. Upon your conviction and your efforts so much depends, and it is a source of satisfaction to be here with Mrs. Johnson, the Vice President's wife, and with the Governor of Texas,—and Senator Carlson—Senator Stennis—most importantly, I think, of Reverend Billy Graham, who has served this cause about which I speak so well here and around the world. He has, I think, transmitted this most important quality of our common commitments to faith in a way which makes all of us particularly proud.

So we are glad to see you this morning, and we appreciate what you are doing.

[*The prayer breakfast of International Christian Leadership, Inc., a nondenominational group of laymen, was held at the Mayflower Hotel in Washington. In his opening words the President referred to Frank Carlson, U.S. Senator from Kansas, who served as chairman of the break- fast; Boyd Leedom, a member of the National Labor Re- lations Board and a former justice of the South Dakota Supreme Court; John W. McCormack, U.S. Representa- tive from Massachusetts and Speaker of the House of Representatives; Earl Warren, Chief Justice of the United States; and Price Daniel, Governor of Texas.]*

★

REMARKS AT THE PAGEANT OF PEACE CEREMONIES
DECEMBER 17, 1862
[*Delivered over radio and television at 5:15 P.M.*]

Ladies and gentlemen, Secretary Udall, members of the clergy:

With the lighting of this tree, which is an old cere- mony in Washington and one which has been among the most important responsibilities of a good many Presidents of the United States, we initiate, in a formal way, the Christmas Season.

We mark the festival of Christmas which is the most sacred and hopeful day in our civilization. For nearly 2,000 years the message of Christmas, the message of peace and good will towards all men, has been the guiding star of our endeavors. This morn- ing I had a meeting at the White House which in- cluded some of our representatives from far off countries in Africa and Asia. They were returning to their posts for the Christmas holidays. Talking with them afterwards, I was struck by the fact that in the far off continents Moslems, Hindus, Bud- dhists, as well as Christians, pause from their labors on the 25th of December to celebrate the birthday of the Prince of Peace. There could be no more striking proof that Christmas is truly the universal

14

holiday of all men. It is the day when all of us dedicate our thoughts to others; when all are reminded that mercy and compassion are the enduring virtues; when all show, by small deeds and large and by acts, that it is more blessed to give than to receive.

It is the day when we remind ourselves that man can and must live in peace with his neighbors and and that it is the peacemakers who are truly blessed. In this year of 1962 we greet each other at Christmas with some special sense of the blessings of peace. This has been a year of peril when the peace has been sorely threatened. But it has been a year when peril was faced and when reason ruled. As a result, we may talk, at this Christmas, just a little bit more confidently of peace on earth, good will to men. As a result, the hopes of the American people are perhaps a little higher. We have much yet to do. We still need to ask that God bless everyone. But yet I think we can enter this season of good will with more than usual joy in our hearts.

And I think all of us extend a special word of gratitude and appreciation to those who serve the United States abroad; to the one million men in uniform who will celebrate this Christmas away from their homes; to those hundreds of young men and women and some older men and women who serve in far off countries in our Peace Corps; to the members of the Foreign Service; to those who work in the various information services, AID agencies, and others who work for us abroad who will celebrate this December 25th thousands of miles from us at sea, on land, and in the air, but with us. It is to them that we offer the best of Christmases and to all of you I send my very best wishes for a blessed and happy Christmas and a peaceful and prosperous New Year.

Thank you.

This (indicating the electric switch) was first

pressed by President Coolidge in 1923 and succeedingly by President Hoover, Vice President Curtis, by President Franklin Roosevelt on many occasions, by President Harry Truman, by President Eisenhower, by Vice President Johnson. I am delighted to be in that illustrious company and we therefore light the tree.

[*The President spoke just before lighting the National Community Christmas Tree at the Pageant of Peace ceremonies on the Ellipse.*]

★

REMARKS AT THE 11TH ANNUAL
PRESIDENTIAL PRAYER BREAKFAST
FEBRUARY 7, 1963

Senator Carlson, Mr. Vice President, Reverend Billy Graham, Mr. Speaker, Mr. Chief Justice, gentlemen:

I am honored to be with you here again this morning. These breakfasts are dedicated to prayer and all of us believe in and need prayer. Of all the thousands of letters that are received in the office of the President of the United States, letters of good will and wishes, none, I am sure, have moved any of the incumbents half so much as those that write that those of us who work here in behalf of the country are remembered in their prayers.

You and I are charged with obligations to serve the Great Republic in years of great crisis. The problems we face are complex; the pressures are immense, and both the perils and the opportunities are greater than any nation ever faced. In such a time, the limits of human endeavor become more apparent than ever. We cannot depend solely on our material wealth, on our military might, on our intellectual skill or physical courage to see us safely through the seas that we must sail in the months and years to come.

Along with all of these we need faith. We need the faith with which our first settlers crossed the sea to carve out a state in the wilderness, a mission they said in the Pilgrims' Compact, the Mayflower Compact, undertaken for the glory of God. We need the faith with which our Founding Fathers proudly proclaimed the independence of this country to what seemed at that time an almost hopeless struggle, pledging their lives, their fortunes, and their sacred honor with a firm reliance on the protection of divine providence. We need the faith which has sustained and guided this Nation for 175 long and short years. We are all builders of the future, and whether we build as public servants or private citizens, whether we build at the national or the local level, whether we build in foreign or domestic affairs, we know the truth of the ancient Psalm, "Except the Lord build the house, they labour in vain that build it."

This morning we pray together; this evening apart. But each morning and each evening, let us remember the advice of my fellow Bostonian, the Reverend Phillips Brooks: "Do not pray for easy lives. Pray to be stronger men! Do not pray for tasks equal to your powers. Pray for powers equal to your tasks."

[*The President spoke first to the gentlemen in the hotel's main ballroom and then to the ladies in the east room.*]

I'm glad to be with you again this morning with the Vice President, Reverend Billy Graham, Dr. Vereide, Senator Carlson, the same quartet that was here last year and the year before.

I think these breakfasts serve a most useful cause in uniting us all on an occasion when we look not to ourselves but to above for assistance. On our way from the last meeting to this, we met two members of Parliament who carried with them a message from Lord Home to this breakfast, in which Lord Home quoted the Bible and said that perhaps the wisest thing that was said in the Bible was the words, "Peace, be still."

I think it's appropriate that we should on occasion be still and consider where we are, where we've been, what we believe in, what we are trying to work for, what we want for our country, what we want our country to be, what our individual responsibilities are, and what our national responsibilities are. This country has carried great responsibilities, particularly in the years since the end of the Second War, and I think that willingness to assume those responsibilities has come in part from the strong religious conviction which must carry with it a sense of responsibility to others if it is genuine, which has marked our country from its earliest beginnings, when the recognition of our obligation to God was stated in nearly every public document, down to the present day.

This is not an occasion for feeling pleased with ourselves, but, rather, it is an occasion for asking for help to continue our work and to do more. This is a country which has this feeling strongly. I mentioned in the other room the letters which I receive, which the members of Congress receive, which the Governors receive, which carry with them by the hundreds the strong commitment to the good life and also the strong feeling of communication which so many of our citizens have with God, and the feeling that we are under His protection. This is, I think, a source of strength to us all.

I want to commend all that you do, not merely

for gathering together this morning, but for all the work and works that make up part of your Christian commitment. I am very proud to be with you.

[*The prayer breakfast of International Christian Leadership, Inc., a nondenominational group of laymen, was held at the Mayflower Hotel in Washington. In his opening words the President referred to Frank Carlson, U.S. Senator from Kansas, who served as chairman of the breakfast; Vice President Lyndon B. Johnson; the Rev. William F. Graham, evangelist; John W. McCormack, Speaker of the House of Representatives; and Earl Warren, Chief Justice of the United States. Later, in his remarks to the ladies, he referred to Dr. Abraham Vereide, Secretary General of the International Council for Christian Leaders.*]

★

ADDRESS AT THE BOSTON COLLEGE
CENTENNIAL CEREMONIES
APRIL 20, 1963

Father Walsh, Your Eminence, Governor Peabody, members of the faculty, ladies and gentlemen:

It is a great pleasure to come back to a city where my accent is considered normal, and where they pronounce the words the way they are spelled!

I take special satisfaction in this day. As the recipient of an honorary degree in 1956 from Boston College, and therefore an instant alumnus, I am particularly pleased to be with all of you on this most felicitous occasion.

This university, or college, as Father Walsh has described, was founded in the darkest days of the Civil War, when this nation was engaged in a climactic struggle to determine whether it would be half slave and half free or all free. And now, 100 years later, after the most intense century perhaps in human history, we are faced with the great question of whether this world will be half slave and half free, or whether it will be all one or the other. And on this occasion, as in 1863, the services of Boston College are still greatly needed.

It is good also to participate in this ceremony which has honored three distinguished citizens of the free world—President Pusey, Father Bunn, and our friend from the world of freedom, Lady Jackson.

Boston College is a hundred years old—old by the life span of men, but young by that of universities. In this week of observance, you have rightly celebrated the achievements of the past, and equally rightly you have turned in a series of discussions by outstanding scholars to the problems of the present and the future. Learned men have been talking here of the knowledge explosion, and in all that they have said I am sure they have implied the heavy present responsibility of institutions like this one. Yet today I want to say a word on the same theme, to impress upon you as urgently as I can the growing and insistent importance of universities in our national life.

I speak of universities because that is what Boston College has long since become. But most of what I say applies to liberal arts colleges as well. My theme is not limited to any one class of universities, public or private, religious or secular. Our national tradition of variety in higher education shows no signs of weakening, and it remains the task of each of our institutions to shape its own role among its differing sisters.

In this hope I am much encouraged by a reading in this past week of the remarkable encyclical, "Pacem in Terris." In its penetrating analysis of today's great problems, of social welfare and human rights, of disarmament and international order and peace, that document surely shows that on the basis of one great faith and its traditions there can be developed counsel on public affairs that is of value to all men and women of good will. As a Catholic I am proud of it; and as an American I have learned from it. It only adds to the impact of this message that it closely matches notable expressions of conviction and aspiration from churchmen of other faiths, as in recent documents of the World Council of Churches, and from outstanding world citizens with no ecclesiastical standing. We are learning to talk the language of progress and peace across the barriers of sect and creed. It seems reasonable to hope that a similar process may be taking place across the quite different barriers of higher learning.

From the office that I hold, in any case, there can be no doubt today of the growing meaning of universities in America. That, of course, is one basic reason for the increasing urgency with which those who care most for the progress of our society are pressing for more adequate programs in higher education and in education generally. It is for this reason that I urge upon everyone here and in this country the pressing need for national attention and a national decision in the national interest upon the national question of education. In at least four ways, the new realities of our day have combined to intensify the focal role of the university in our Nation's life.

First, and perhaps most obvious, the whole world has come to our doorstep and the universities must be its student. In the strange geometry of modern politics, the distant Congo can be as close to us as Canada, and Canada, itself, is worth more attention than we have sometimes given. Cultures not our own press for understanding. Crises we did not create require our participation. Accelerating change is the one universal human prospect. The universities must help.

Second, there is indeed an explosion of knowledge and its outward limits are not yet in sight. In some fields, progress seems very fast; in others, distressingly slow. It is no tribute to modern science to jump lightly to the conclusion that all its secrets of particle physics, of molecular life, of heredity, of outer space, are now within easy reach. The truth is more massive and less magical. It is that wherever we turn, in defense, in space, in medicine, in industry, in agriculture, and most of all in basic science, itself, the requirement is for better work, deeper understanding, higher education. And while I have framed this comment in the terms of the natural sciences, I insist, as do all who live in this field, that at every level of learning there must be an equal concern for history, for letters and the arts, and for man as a social being in the widest meaning of Aristotle's phrase. This also is the work of the university.

And third, as the world presses in and knowledge presses out, the role of the interpreter grows. Men can no longer know everything themselves; the 20th century has no universal man. All men today must learn to know through one another—to judge across their own ignorance—to comprehend at second hand. These arts are not easily learned. Those who would practice them must develop intensity of perception, variety of mental activity, and the habit of open concern for truth in all its forms. Where can we expect to find a training ground for this modern maturity, if not in our universities?

Fourth and finally, these new requirements strengthen still further what has always been a fundamental element in the life of American colleges and universities—that they should be dedicated to "the Nation's service." The phrase is Woodrow Wilson's, and no one has discussed its meaning better. What he said in 1896 is more relevant today than ever before, and I close with a quotation from him.

I offer it to you with renewed congratulations, and in the confident hope that as the second century opens, Boston College will continue to respond—as she did in her beginnings—to the new needs of the age.

"It is not learning," said President Wilson, "but the spirit of service that will give a college place in the public annals of the Nation." "It is indispensable," he said, "if it is to do its right service, that the air of affairs should be admitted to all its classrooms . . . the air of the world's transactions, the consciousness of the solidarity of the race, the sense of the duty of man toward man . . . the promise and the hope that shine in the face of all knowledge. . . . The days of glad expansion are gone, our life grows tense and difficult; our resource for the future lies in careful thought, providence, and a wise economy; and the school must be of the Nation."

Boston College for 100 years has been of the Nation and so it will be for the next hundred.

Thank you.

[*The President spoke at 2:45 P.M. in Alumni Stadium on the college campus at Newton, Mass. His opening words referred to the Reverend Michael P. Walsh, S.J., President of Boston College; His Eminence Richard Cardinal Cushing, Archbishop of Boston; and Governor Endicott Peabody of Massachusetts. Later he referred to Nathan N. Pusey, President of Harvard University; the Very Reverend Edward B. Bunn, S.J., President of Georgetown University; and Lady Barbara Ward Jackson, noted British writer—all of whom were awarded honorary degrees by Boston College.*]

President Anderson, members of the faculty, board of trustees, distinguished guests, my old colleague, Senator Bob Byrd, who has earned his degree through many years of attending night law school, while I am earning mine in the next 30 minutes, ladies and gentlemen:

It is with great pride that I participate in this ceremony of the American University, sponsored by the Methodist Church, founded by Bishop John Fletcher Hurst, and first opened by President Woodrow Wilson in 1914. This is a young and growing university, but it has already fulfilled Bishop Hurst's enlightened hope for the study of history and public affairs in a city devoted to the making of history and to the conduct of the public's business. By sponsoring this institution of higher learning for all who wish to learn, whatever their color or their creed, the Methodists of this area and the Nation deserve the Nation's thanks, and I commend all those who are today graduating.

Professor Woodrow Wilson once said that every man sent out from a university should be a man of his nation as well as a man of his time, and I am confident that the men and women who carry the honor of graduating from this institution will continue to give from their lives, from their talents, a high measure of public service and public support.

"There are few earthly things more beautiful than a university," wrote John Masefield, in his tribute to English universities—and his words are equally true today. He did not refer to spires and towers, to campus greens and ivied walls. He admired the splendid beauty of the university, he said, because it was "a place where those who hate ignorance may

24

strive to know, where those who perceive truth may strive to make others see."

I have, therefore, chosen this time and this place to discuss a topic on which ignorance too often abounds and the truth is too rarely perceived—yet it is the most important topic on earth: world peace.

What kind of peace do I mean? What kind of peace do we seek? Not a Pax Americana enforced on the world by American weapons of war. Not the peace of the grave or the security of the slave. I am talking about genuine peace, the kind of peace that makes life on earth worth living, the kind that enables men and nations to grow and to hope and to build a better life for their children—not merely peace for Americans but peace for all men and women—not merely peace for our time but peace for all times.

I speak of peace because of the new face of war. Total war makes no sense in an age when great powers can maintain large and relatively invulnerable nuclear forces and refuse to surrender without resort to those forces. It makes no sense in an age when a single nuclear weapon contains almost ten times the explosive force delivered by all of the allied air forces in the Second World War. It makes no sense in an age when the deadly poisons produced by a nuclear exchange would be carried by wind and water and soil and seed to the far corners of the globe and to generations yet unborn.

Today the expenditures of billions of dollars every year on weapons acquired for the purpose of making sure we never need to use them is essential to keeping the peace. But surely the acquisition of such idle stockpiles—which can only destroy and never create —is not the only, much less the most efficient, means of assuring the peace.

I speak of peace, therefore, as the necessary rational end of rational man. I realize that the pursuit

of peace is not as dramatic as the pursuit of war—
and frequently the words of the pursuer fall on deaf
ears. But we have no more urgent task.

Some say that it is useless to speak of world peace
or world law or world disarmament—and that it
will be useless until the leaders of the Soviet Union
adopt a more enlightened attitude. I hope they do.
I believe we can help them do it. But I also believe
that we must reexamine our own attitude—as individuals and as a Nation—for our attitude is as essential as theirs. And every graduate of this school,
every thoughtful citizen who despairs of war and
wishes to bring peace, should begin by looking in-
ward—by examining his own attitude toward the
possibilities of peace, toward the Soviet Union, toward the course of the cold war and toward freedom
and peace here at home.

First: Let us examine our attitude toward peace
itself. Too many of us think it is impossible. Too
many think it is unreal. But that is a dangerous,
defeatist belief. It leads to the conclusion that war
is inevitable—that mankind is doomed—that we are
gripped by forces we cannot control.

We need not accept that view. Our problems are
manmade—therefore, they can be solved by man.
And man can be as big as he wants. No problem of
human destiny is beyond human beings. Man's
reason and spirit have often solved the seemingly
unsolvable—and we believe they can do it again.

I am not referring to the absolute, infinite concept of universal peace and good will of which some
fantasies and fanatics dream. I do not deny the
value of hopes and dreams but I merely invite dis-
couragement and incredulity by making that our
only and immediate goal.

Let us focus instead on a more practical, more at-
tainable peace—based not on a sudden revolution
in human nature but on a gradual evolution in

human institutions—on a series of concrete actions and effective agreements which are in the interest of all concerned. There is no single, simple key to this peace—no grand or magic formula to be adopted by one or two powers. Genuine peace must be the product of many nations, the sum of many acts. It must be dynamic, not static, changing to meet the challenge of each new generation. For peace is a process—a way of solving problems.

With such a peace, there will still be quarrels and conflicting interests, as there are within families and nations. World peace, like community peace, does not require that each man love his neighbor—it requires only that they live together in mutual tolerance, submitting their disputes to a just and peaceful settlement. And history teaches us that enmities between nations, as between individuals, do not last forever. However fixed our likes and dislikes may seem, the tide of time and events will often bring surprising changes in the relations between nations and neighbors.

So let us persevere. Peace need not be impracticable, and war need not be inevitable. By defining our goal more clearly, by making it seem more manageable and less remote, we can help all peoples to see it, to draw hope from it, and to move irresistibly toward it.

Second: Let us reexamine our attitude toward the Soviet Union. It is discouraging to think that their leaders may actually believe what their propagandists write. It is discouraging to read a recent authoritative Soviet text on *Military Strategy* and find, on page after page, wholly baseless and incredible claims—such as the allegation that "American imperialist circles are preparing to unleash different types of wars . . . that there is a very real threat of a preventive war being unleashed by American imperialists against the Soviet Union . . . (and

27

that) the political aims of the American imperialists are to enslave economically and politically the European and other capitalist countries . . . (and) to achieve world domination . . . by means of aggressive wars."

Truly, as it was written long ago: "The wicked flee when no man pursueth." Yet it is sad to read these Soviet statements—to realize the extent of the gulf between us. But it is also a warning—a warning to the American people not to fall into the same trap as the Soviets, not to see only a distorted and desperate view of the other side, not to see conflict as inevitable, accomodation as impossible, and communication as nothing more than an exchange of theses.

No government or social system is so evil that its people must be considered as lacking in virtue. As Americans, we find communism profoundly repugnant as a negation of personal freedom and dignity. But we can still hail the Russian people for their many achievements—in science and space, in economic and industrial growth, in culture and in acts of courage.

Among the many traits the people of our two countries have in common, none is stronger than our mutual abhorrence of war. Almost unique, among the major world powers, we have never been at war with each other. And no nation in the history of battle ever suffered more than the Soviet Union suffered in the course of the Second World War. At least twenty million lost their lives. Countless millions of homes and farms were burned or sacked. A third of the nation's territory, including nearly two thirds of its industrial base, was turned into a wasteland—a loss equivalent to the devastation of this country east of Chicago.

Today, should total war ever break out again— no matter how—our two countries would become the primary targets. It is an ironic but accurate fact that the two strongest powers are the two in the most danger of devastation. All we have built, all we have worked for, would be destroyed in the first 24 hours. And even in the cold war, which brings burdens and dangers to so many countries, including this Nation's closest allies—our two countries bear the heaviest burdens. For we are both devoting massive sums of money to weapons that could be better devoted to combating ignorance, poverty, and disease. We are both caught up in a vicious and dangerous cycle in which suspicion on the one side breeds suspicion on the other, and new weapons beget counterweapons.

In short, both the United States and its allies, and the Soviet Union and its allies, have a mutually deep interest in a just and genuine peace and in halting the arms race. Agreements to this end are in the interests of the Soviet Union as well as ours—and even the most hostile nations can be relied upon to accept and keep those treaty obligations, and only those treaty obligations, which are in their own interest.

So, let us not be blind to our differences—but let us also direct attention to our common interests and to the means by which those differences can be resolved. And if we cannot end now our differences, at least we can help make the world safe for diversity. For, in the final analysis, our most basic common link is that we all inhabit this small planet. We all breathe the same air. We all cherish our children's future. And we are all mortal.

Third: Let us reexamine our attitude toward the cold war, remembering that we are not engaged in a debate, seeking to pile up debating points. We must deal with the world as it is, not as it might have been had the history of the last 18 years been different.

We must, therefore, persevere in the search for peace in the hope that constructive changes within the Communist bloc might bring within reach solutions which now seem beyond us. We must conduct our affairs in such a way that it becomes in the Communists' interest to agree on a genuine peace. Above all, while defending our own vital interests, nuclear powers must avert those confrontations which bring an adversary to a choice of either a humiliating retreat or a nuclear war. To adopt that kind of course in the nuclear age would be evidence only of the bankruptcy of our policy—or of a collective death-wish for the world.

To secure these ends, America's weapons are non-provocative, carefully controlled, designed to deter, and capable of selective use. Our military forces are committed to peace and disciplined in self-restraint. Our diplomats are instructed to avoid unnecessary irritants and purely rhetorical hostility.

For we can seek a relaxation of tensions without relaxing our guard. And, for our part, we do not need to use threats to prove that we are resolute. We do not need to jam foreign broadcasts out of fear our faith will be eroded. We are unwilling to impose our system on any unwilling people—but we are willing and able to engage in peaceful competition with any people on earth.

Meanwhile, we seek to strengthen the United Nations, to help solve its financial problems, to make it a more effective instrument for peace, to develop it into a genuine world security system—a system capable of resolving disputes on the basis of law, of insuring the security of the large and the small, and of creating conditions under which arms can finally be abolished.

At the same time we seek to keep peace inside the non-Communist world, where many nations, all of them our friends, are divided over issues which weaken Western unity, which invite Communist intervention or which threaten to erupt into war. Our efforts in West New Guinea, in the Congo, in the Middle East, and in the Indian sub-continent, have been persistent and patient despite criticism from both sides. We have also tried to set an example for others—by seeking to adjust small but significant differences with our own closest neighbors in Mexico and Canada.

Speaking of other nations, I wish to make one point clear. We are bound to many nations by alliances. Those alliances exist because our concern and theirs substantially overlap. Our commitment to defend Western Europe and West Berlin, for example, stands undiminished because of the identity of our vital interests. The United States will make no deal with the Soviet Union at the expense of other nations and other peoples, not merely because they are our partners, but also because their interests and ours converge.

Our interests converge, however, not only in defending the frontiers of freedom, but in pursuing the paths of peace. It is our hope—and the purpose of allied policies—to convince the Soviet Union that she, too, should let each nation choose its own future, so long as that choice does not interfere with the choice of others. The Communist drive to impose their political and economic system on others is the primary cause of world tension today. For there can be no doubt that, if all nations could refrain from interfering in the self-determination of others, the peace would be much more assured.

This will require a new effort to achieve world law—a new context for world discussions. It will require increased understanding between the Soviets and ourselves. And increased understanding will require increased contact and communication. One step in this direction is the proposed arrangement for a direct line between Moscow and Washington, to avoid on each side the dangerous delays, misunderstandings, and misreadings of the other's actions which might occur at a time of crisis.

We have been talking in Geneva about our first-step measures of arms control, designed to limit the intensity of the arms race and to reduce the risks of accidental war. Our primary long-range interest in Geneva, however, is general and complete disarmament—designed to take place by stages, permitting parallel political developments to build the new institutions of peace which would take the place of arms. The pursuit of disarmament has been the effort of this Government since the 1920's. It has been urgently sought by the past three administrations. And however dim the prospects may be today, we intend to continue this effort—to continue it in order that all countries, including our own, can better grasp what the problems and possibilities of disarmament are.

The one major area of these negotiations where the end is in sight, yet where a fresh start is badly needed, is in a treaty to outlaw nuclear tests. The conclusion of such a treaty, so near and yet so far, would check the spiraling arms race in one of its most dangerous areas. It would place the nuclear powers in a position to deal more effectively with one of the greatest hazards which man faces in 1963, the further spread of nuclear arms. It would increase our security—it would decrease the possibilities of war. Surely this goal is sufficiently important to require our steady pursuit, yielding neither to the temptation to give up the whole effort nor the temptation to give up our insistence on vital and responsible safeguards.

I am taking this opportunity, therefore, to announce two important decisions in this regard.

First: Chairman Khrushchev, Prime Minister

Macmillan, and I have agreed that high-level discussions will shortly begin in Moscow looking toward early agreement on a comprehensive test ban treaty. Our hopes must be tempered with the caution of history—but with our hopes go the hopes of all mankind.

Second: To make clear our good faith and solemn convictions on the matter, I now declare that the United States does not propose to conduct nuclear tests in the atmosphere so long as other states do not do so. We will not be the first to resume. Such a declaration is no substitute for a formal binding treaty, but I hope it will help us achieve one. Nor would such a treaty be a substitute for disarmament, but I hope it will help us achieve it.

Finally, my fellow Americans, let us examine our attitude toward peace and freedom here at home. The quality and spirit of our own society must justify and support our efforts abroad. We must show it in the dedication of our own lives—as many of you who are graduating today will have a unique opportunity to do, by serving without pay in the Peace Corps abroad or in the proposed National Service Corps here at home.

But wherever we are, we must all, in our daily lives, live up to the age-old faith that freedom and peace walk together. In too many of our cities today, the peace is not secure because freedom is incomplete.

It is the responsibility of the executive branch at all levels of government—local, State, and National —to provide and protect that freedom for all our citizens by all means within their authority. It is the responsibility of the legislative branch at all levels, wherever that authority is not now adequate, to make it adequate. And it is the responsibility of all citizens of all sections of this country to respect the rights of all others and to respect the law of the land.

All this is not unrelated to world peace. "When

a man's ways please the Lord," the Scriptures tell us, "he maketh even his enemies to be at peace with him." And is not peace, in the last analysis, basically a matter of human rights—the right to live out our lives without fear of devastation—the right to breathe air as nature provided it—the right of future generations to a healthy existence?

While we proceed to safeguard our national interests, let us also safeguard human interests. And the elimination of war and arms is clearly in the interest of both. No treaty, however much it may be to the advantage of all, however tightly it may be worded, can provide absolute security against the risks of deception and evasion. But it can—if it is sufficiently effective in its enforcement and if it is sufficiently in the interest of its signers—offer far more security and far fewer risks than an unabated, uncontrolled, unpredictable arms race.

The United States, as the world knows, will never start a war. We do not want a war. We do not now expect a war. This generation of Americans has already had enough—more than enough—of war and hate and oppression. We shall be prepared if others wish it. We shall be alert to try to stop it. But we shall also do our part to build a world of peace where the weak are safe and the strong are just. We are not helpless before that task or hopeless of its success. Confident and unafraid, we labor on—not toward a strategy of annihilation but toward a strategy of peace.

[*The President spoke at the John M. Reeves Athletic Field on the Campus of the American University after being awarded an honorary degree of doctor of laws. In his opening words he referred to Hurst R. Anderson, president of the university, and Robert C. Byrd, U.S. Senator from West Virginia.*]

Monsignor, Rectors:

I want to express a very warm welcome to all of you, and we take a good deal of pride and satisfaction in your having chosen, I think, for the first time, to come to Washington to hold this meeting.

The purposes of this meeting, which I understand are to concern yourselves with the problem of education in the developing countries and also with the relationship of Western civilization, Western culture, Western religious life with the East, with oriental civilization and culture—I think both of these purposes are most worthwhile.

Knowledge is power, and I think the events of the past years have shown that in a very dramatic way.

I am particularly interested in the progress we can make in the developing countries—Latin America, Africa, and Asia.

The need for trained men and women in all the disciplines of life, constantly increasing as technology and science expand our horizons, and the relatively small educated elite which we find in these countries on whom heavy burdens have been placed, I think, indicate how essential it is in the sixties that the universities of the West, particularly in the highly developed countries, concentrate their attention on expanding education, indicating that education is not merely a means and an end, and not merely a technique, but also a way to the good life which is a way to a more secure and afterlife.

I recognize how difficult it is to maintain a free society under the best of conditions. We in the United States have many problems. With all the advantages that nature—and also the qualities of self-restraint and discipline which have been developed in our people, we recognize how difficult it is to sustain the democratic system.

Western Europe has also had its adverse experiences, but yet they have a broad educational base, a long religious tradition, a great cultural record and yet they have found that the self-discipline which goes with self-government is difficult to maintain.

If we in the West find it so difficult, imagine how complicated it is for the newly developing countries which lack this long tradition, which lack this happy balance of economic and political power which we have been able to develop in this country. So this makes your job most important, this meeting most significant.

We are very proud of what you are doing, of the long tradition which some of your universities represent. We take a good deal of pride in the schools which have been built in this country, and what I am most impressed by is, instead of talking about the rather esoteric subjects which sometimes occupy the attention of educators, that in 1963 you are talking about two very important problems: the problem of education in the developing world, and the problem of our relations with the East. So it shows that even though Salamanca and Louvain, and all the rest, may go back hundreds and hundreds of years, in 1963 you are looking to the future.

We are glad to have you here.

[*The President spoke at 10:00* A.M. *in the garden at the White House. His opening words "Monsignor, Rectors" referred to the Right Reverend William J. McDonald, president of the Federation, and to the rectors of 50 Catholic universities in 21 countries.*]

Senator Moss, my old colleague in the United States Senate, your distinguished Senator Moss, President McKay, Mr. Brown, Secretary Udall, Governor, Mr. Rawlings, ladies and gentlemen:

I appreciate your welcome, and I am very proud to be back in this historic building and have an opportunity to say a few words on some matters which concern me as President, and I hope concern you as citizens. The fact is, I take strength and hope in seeing this monument, hearing its story re-told by Ted Moss, and recalling how this state was built, and what it started with, and what it has now.

Of all the stories of American pioneers and settlers, none is more inspiring than the Mormon trail. The qualities of the founders of this community are the qualities that we seek in America, the qualities which we like to feel this country has, courage, patience, faith, self-reliance, perseverance, and, above all, an unflagging determination to see the right prevail.

I came on this trip to see the United States, and I can assure you that there is nothing more encouraging for any of us who work in Washington than to have a chance to fly across this United States, and drive through it, and see what a great country it is, and come to understand somewhat better how this country has been able for so many years to carry so many burdens in so many parts of the world.

The primary reason for my trip was conservation, and I include in conservation first our human resources and then our natural resources, and I think this State can take perhaps its greatest pride and its greatest satisfaction for what it has done, not in the field of conservation and the development of natural resources, but what you have done to educate your children. This State has a higher percentage per capita of population of its boys and girls who finish high school and then go to college.

Of all the waste in the United States in the 1960's, none is worse than to have 8 or 9 million boys and girls who will drop out, statistics tell us, drop out of school before they have finished, come into the labor market unprepared at the very time when machines are taking the place of men and women—9 million of them. We have a large minority of our population who have not even finished the sixth grade, and here in this richest of all countries, the country which spreads the doctrine of freedom and hope around the globe, we permit our most valuable resource, our young people, their talents to be wasted by leaving their schools.

So I think we have to save them. I think we have to insist that our children be educated to the limit of their talents, not just in your State, or in Massachusetts, but all over the United States. Thomas Jefferson and John Adams, who developed the Northwest Ordinance, which put so much emphasis on education—Thomas Jefferson once said that any nation which expected to be ignorant and free, hopes for what never was and never will be. So I hope we can conserve this resource.

The other is the natural resource of our country, particularly the land west of the 100th parallel, where the rain comes 15 or 20 inches a year. This State knows that the control of water is the secret of the development of the West, and whether we use it for power, or for irrigation, or for whatever purpose, no drop of water west of the 100th parallel should flow to the ocean without being used. And to do that requires the dedicated commitment of the people of the States of the West, working with the people of all the United States who have such an important equity in the richness of this part of the country. So that we must do also.

As Theodore and Franklin Roosevelt and Gifford Pinchot did it in years past, we must do it in the 1960's and 1970's. We will triple the population of this country in the short space of 60 or 70 years, and we want those who come after us to have the same rich inheritance that we find now in the United States. This is the reason for the trip, but it is not what I wanted to speak about tonight.

I want to speak about the responsibility that I feel the United States has not in this country, but abroad, and I see the closest interrelationship between the strength of the United States here at home and the strength of the United States around the world. There is one great natural development here in the United States which has had in its own way a greater effect upon the position and influence and prestige of the United States, almost, than any other act we have done. Do you know what it is? It is the Tennessee Valley. Nearly every leader of every new emerging country that comes to the United States wants to go to New York, to Washington, and the Tennessee Valley, because they want to see what we were able to do with the most poverty-ridden section of the United States in the short space of 30 years, by the wise management of our resources.

What happens here in this country affects the security of the United States and the cause of freedom around the globe. If this is a strong, vital, and vigorous society, the cause of freedom will be strong and vital and vigorous.

I know that many of you in this State and other States sometimes wonder where we are going and why the United States should be so involved in so many affairs, in so many countries all around the globe. If our task on occasion seems hopeless, if we despair of ever working our will on the other 94 percent of the world population, then let us remember that the Mormons of a century ago were a persecuted and prosecuted minority, harried from place to place, the victims of violence and occasionally murder, while today, in the short space of 100 years, their faith and works are known and respected the world around, and their voices heard in the highest councils of this country.

As the Mormons succeeded, so America can succeed, if we will not give up or turn back. I realize that the burdens are heavy and I realize that there is a great temptation to urge that we relinquish them, that we have enough to do here in the United States, and we should not be so busy around the globe. The fact of the matter is that we, this generation of Americans, are the first generation of our country ever to be involved in affairs around the globe. From the beginning of this country, from the days of Washington, until the Second World War, this country lived an isolated existence. Through most of our history we were an unaligned country, an uncommitted nation, a neutralist nation. We were by statute as well as by desire. We had believed that we could live behind our two oceans in safety and prosperity in a comfortable distance from the rest of the world.

The end of isolation consequently meant a wrench with the very lifeblood, the very spine, of the Nation. Yet, as time passed, we came to see that the end of isolation was not such a terrible error or evil after all. We came to see that it was the inevitable result of growth, the economic growth, the military growth, and the cultural growth of the United States. No nation so powerful and so dynamic and as rich as our own could hope to live in isolation from other nations, especially at a time when science and technology was making the world so small.

It took Brigham Young and his followers 108 days to go from Winter Quarters, Nebraska, to the valley of the Great Salt Lake. It takes 30 minutes for a missile to go from one continent to another. We did not seek to become a world power. This position was thrust upon us by events. But we became one just the same, and I am proud that we did.

I can well understand the attraction of those earlier days. Each one of us has moments of longing for the past, but two world wars have clearly shown us, try as we may, that we cannot turn our back on the world outside. If we do, we jeopardize our economic well-being, we jeopardize our political stability, we jeopardize our physical safety.

To turn away now is to abandon the world to those whose ambition is to destroy a free society. To yield these burdens up after having carried them for more than 20 years is to surrender the freedom of our country inevitably, for without the United States, the chances of freedom surviving, let alone prevailing around the globe, are nonexistent.

Americans have come a long way in accepting in a short time the necessity of world involvement, but the strain of this involvement remains and we find it all over the country. I see it in the letters that come to my desk every day. We find ourselves entangled with apparently unanswerable problems in unpronounceable places. We discover that our enemy in one decade is our ally the next. We find ourselves committed to governments whose actions we cannot often approve, assisting societies with principles very different from our own.

The burdens of maintaining an immense military establishment with one million Americans serving outside our frontiers, of financing a far-flung program of development assistance, of conducting a complex and baffling diplomacy, all weigh heavily upon us and cause some to counsel retreat. The world is full of contradiction and confusion, and our policy seems to have lost the black and white clarity of simpler times when we remembered the Maine and went to war.

It is little wonder, then, in this confusion, we look back to the old days with nostalgia. It is little wonder that there is a desire in the country to go back to the time when our Nation lived alone. It is little wonder that we increasingly want an end to entangling alliances, an end to all help to foreign countries, a cessation of diplomatic relations with countries or states whose principles we dislike, that we get the United Nations out of the United States, and the United States out of the United Nations, and that we retreat to our own hemisphere, or even within our own boundaries, to take refuge behind a wall of force.

This is an understandable effort to recover an old feeling of simplicity, yet in world affairs, as in all other aspects of our lives, the days of the quiet past are gone forever. Science and technology are irreversible. We cannot return to the day of the sailing schooner or the covered wagon, even if we wished. And if this Nation is to survive and succeed in the real world of today, we must acknowledge the realities of the world; and it is those realities that I mention now.

We must first of all recognize that we cannot remake the world simply by our own command. When we cannot even bring all of our own people into full citizenship without acts of violence, we can understand how much harder it is to control events beyond our borders.

Every nation has its own traditions, its own values, its own aspirations. Our assistance from time to time can help other nations preserve their independence and advance their growth, but we cannot remake them in our own image. We cannot enact their laws, nor can we operate their governments or dictate our policies.

Second, we must recognize that every nation determines its policies in terms of its own interests. "No nation," George Washington wrote, "is to be trusted farther than it is bound by its interest; and no prudent statesman or politician will depart from this." National interest is more powerful than ideology, and the recent developments within the Communist empire show this very clearly. Friendship, as Palmerston said, may rise or wane, but interests endure.

The United States has rightly determined, in the years since 1945 under three different administrations, that our interest, our national security, the interest of the United States of America, is best served by preserving and protecting a world of diversity in which no one power or no one combination of powers can threaten the security of the United States. The reason that we moved so far into the world was our fear that at the end of the war, and particularly when China became Communist, that Japan and Germany would collapse, and these two countries which had so long served as a barrier to the Soviet advance, and the Russian advance after that, would open up a wave of conquest of all of Europe and all of Asia, and then the balance of power turning against us we would finally be isolated and ultimately destroyed. That is what we have been engaged in for 18 years, to prevent that happening, to prevent any one monolithic power having sufficient force to destroy the United States.

For that reason we support the alliances in Latin America; for that reason we support NATO to protect the security of Western Europe; for that reason we joined SEATO to protect the security of Asia— so that neither Russia nor China could control Europe and Asia, and if they could not control Europe and Asia, then our security was assured. This is what we have been involved in doing. And however dangerous and hazardous it may be, and however close it may take us to the brink on occasion, which it has, and however tired we may get of our involvements with these governments so far away, we have one simple central theme of American foreign policy which all of us must recognize, because it is a policy which we must continue to follow, and that is to support the independence of nations so that one bloc cannot gain sufficient power to finally overcome us. There is no mistaking the vital interest of the United States in what goes on around the world. Therefore, accepting what George Washington said here, I realize that what George Washington said about no intangling alliances has been ended by science and technology and danger.

And third, we must recognize that foreign policy in the modern world does not lend itself to easy, simple black and white solution. If we were to have diplomatic relations only with those countries whose principles we approved of, we would have relations with very few countries in a very short time. If we were to withdraw our assistance from all governments who are run differently from our own, we would relinquish half the world immediately to our adversaries. If we were to treat foreign policy as merely a medium for delivering self-righteous sermons to supposedly inferior people, we would give up all thought of world influence or world leadership.

For the purpose of foreign policy is not to provide an outlet for our own sentiments of hope or indignation; it is to shape real events in a real world. We cannot adopt a policy which says that if something does not happen, or others do not do exactly what we wish, we will return to "Fortress America." That is the policy in this changing world of retreat, not of strength.

More important, to adopt a black or white, all or nothing policy subordinates our interest to our irritations. Its actual consequences would be fatal to our security. If we were to resign from the United Nations, break off with all countries of whom we disapprove, end foreign aid and assistance to those countries in an attempt to keep them free, call for the resumption of atmospheric nuclear testing, and turn our back on the rest of mankind, we would not only be abandoning America's influence in the world, we would be inviting a Communist expansion which every Communist power would so greatly welcome. And all of the effort of so many Americans for 18 years would be gone with the wind. Our policy under those conditions, in this dangerous world, would not have much deterrent effect in a world where nations determined to be free could no longer count on the United States.

Such a policy of retreat would be folly if we had our backs to the wall. It is surely even greater folly at a time when more realistic, more responsible, more affirmative policies have wrought such spectacular results. For the most striking thing about our world in 1963 is the extent to which the tide of history has begun to flow in the direction of freedom. To renounce the world of freedom now, to abandon those who share our commitment, and to retire into lonely and not so splendid isolation, would be to give communism the one hope which, in this twilight of disappointment for them, might repair their divisions and rekindle their hopes.

For after some gains in the fifties the Communist offensive, which claimed to be riding the tide of historic inevitability, has been thwarted and turned back in recent months. Indeed, the whole theory of historic inevitability, the belief that all roads must lead to communism, sooner or later, has been shattered by the determination of those who believe that men and nations will pursue a variety of roads, that each nation will evolve according to its own traditions and its own aspirations, and that the world of the future will have room for a diversity of economic systems, political creeds, religious faiths, united by respect for each other, and loyalty to world order.

Those forces of diversity which served Mr. Washington's national interest—those forces of diversity are on the ascendency today, even within the Communist empire itself. And our policy at this point should be to give the forces of diversity, as opposed to the forces of uniformity, which our adversaries espouse, every chance, every possible support. That is why our assistance program, so much maligned, of assisting countries to maintain their freedom, I believe, is important.

This country has seen all of the hardship and the grief that has come to us by the loss of one country in this hemisphere, Cuba. How many other countries must be lost if the United States decides to end the programs that are helping these people, who are getting poorer every year, who have none of the resources of this great country, who look to us for help, but on the other hand in cases look to the Communists for example?

That is why I think this program is important. It is a means of assisting those who want to be free, and in the final analysis it serves the United States in a very real sense. That is why the United Nations is important, not because it can solve all these problems in this imperfect world, but it does give us a means, in those great moments of crisis, and in the last two and one-half years we have had at least three, when the Soviet Union and the United States were almost face to face on a collision course—it does give us a means of providing, as it has in the Congo, as it now is on the border of the Yemen, as it most recently was in a report of the United Nations at Malaysia—it does give a means to mobilize the opinion of the world to prevent an atomic disaster which would destroy us all wherever we might live.

That is why the test ban treaty is important as a first step, perhaps to be disappointed, perhaps to find ourselves ultimately set back, but at least in 1963 the United States committed itself, and the Senate of the United States, by an overwhelming vote, to one chance to end the radiation and the possibilities of burning.

It may be, as I have said, that we may fail, but anyone who bothers to look at the true destructive power of the atom today and what we and the Soviet Union could do to each other and the world in an hour and in a day, and to Western Europe—I passed over yesterday the Little Big Horn where General Custer was slain, a massacre which has lived in history, 400 or 500 men. We are talking about 300 million men and women in 24 hours.

I think it is wise to take a first step to lessen the possibility of that happening. And that is why our diplomacy is important. For the forces making for diversity are to be found everywhere where people are, even within the Communist empire, and it is our obligation to encourage those forces wherever they may be found. Hard and discouraging questions remain in Vietnam, in Cuba, in Laos, the Congo, all around the globe. The ordeal of the emerging nations has just begun. The control of nuclear weapons is still incomplete. The areas of potential friction, the chances of collision, still exist.

But in every one of these areas the position of the United States, I believe, is happier and safer when history is going for us rather than when it is going against us. And we have history going for us today, but history is what men make it. The future is what men make it.

We cannot fulfill our vision and our commitment and our interest in a free and diverse future without unceasing vigilance, devotion, and, most of all, perseverance, a willingness to stay with it, a willingness to do with fatigue, a willingness not to accept easy answers, but instead, to maintain the burden, as the people of this State have done for 100 years, and as the United States must do the rest of this century until finally we live in a peaceful world.

Therefore, I think this country will continue its commitments to support the world of freedom, for as we discharge that commitment we are heeding the command which Brigham Young heard from the Lord more than a century ago, the command he conveyed to his followers, "Go as pioneers . . . to a land of peace."

Thank you.

[*In his opening words the President referred to Frank E. Moss, U.S. Senator from Utah; David O. McKay, President of the Mormon Church, and Hugh B. Brown, his First Counselor; Stewart L. Udall, Secretary of the Interior; George Dewey Clyde, Governor of Utah; and Calvin W. Rawlings of Salt Lake City, Democratic National Committeeman for Utah.*]

★

REMARKS AT THE DINNER OF THE PROTESTANT COUNCIL OF THE CITY OF NEW YORK
NOVEMBER 8, 1963

Doctor Kinsolving, Dr. Sockman, Rev. Potter, Father Morgan, Rabbi Rosenbloom, Mr. Mayor,

Governor Stevenson, Mr. Champion, Mr. Leidesdorf, distinguished guests, ladies and gentlemen:

I had wondered what I would do when I retired from the Presidency, whenever that time might come, but Dr. Sockman was the first man to suggest work as challenging as the Presidency in becoming chairman of the Protestant Council's annual dinner, and I am very grateful to him.

I also regret very much that another honored guest of this dinner on a previous occasion is not with us tonight. I follow his career with more interest than he might imagine. In his quest for the Presidency, Governor Rockefeller follows the example of other distinguished New Yorkers—Wendell Willkie, Thomas Dewey, Richard Nixon, and I wish him some margin of success.

I am gratified to receive this award from the Council, and I am impressed by what you are doing here in the city, and I think that the words of Reverend Potter bear very careful reflection by us all. The United States is not in the position which England was when Benjamin Disraeli described it as: two nations divided, the rich and the poor. This is generally a prosperous country, but there is a stream of poverty that runs across the United States which is not exposed to the lives of a good many of us and, therefore, we are relatively unaware of it except statistically. It is concentrated to a large measure in the large cities from which, as he said, so many people are moving out. It is concentrated in some of our rural areas.

The New York Times 2 weeks ago, I think, had an article by Mr. Bigart on the desperate poverty in several rural counties of eastern Kentucky—schools which were without windows, sometimes with occasional teachers, counties without resources to distribute the surplus food that we make available. And what is true in some of the older coal mining areas of the United States is very true in our cities. We see it in some of our statistics, where we have a mental retardation rate for our children of three times that of Sweden, where we have an infant mortality rate behind half the countries of Europe, plus we have about 8 million boys and girls in this decade who will drop out of school, and a good many of them out of work. And this Council, and the religious leaders of the Catholic faith and Jewish faith have a great responsibility not only for the moral life of the community, but also for the well-being of those who have been left behind.

We are attempting, in cooperation with the State and the city, as Reverend Potter described, to carry out a pilot program here in the city of New York, but it is only a beginning, and there are hundreds of thousands without resources, and we have a responsibility to all of them. We have it in Washington. Schools were integrated a few years ago. About half the population of Washington is Negro. Today about 85 percent of the children in the schools of Washington are Negro. Other whites who are more prosperous generally have moved away and left the problem behind. So I commend this Council for its concern for the Family of Man here in the city of New York, and I hope its efforts will be matched by others in other cities across the country, and that we will remember in this very rich, constantly increasing prosperity that there are some for whom we have a responsibility.

I want to speak tonight very briefly, however, about the Family of Man beyond the United States. Just as the Family of Man is not limited to a single race or religion, neither can it be limited to a single city or country. The Family of Man is more than 3 billion strong. It lives in more than 100 nations. Most of its members are not white. Most of them are not Christians. Most of them know nothing about free enterprise or due process of law or the Australian ballot.

If our society is to promote the Family of Man, let us realize the magnitude of our task. This is a sobering assignment. For the Family of Man in the world of today is not faring very well.

The members of a family should be at peace with one another, but they are not. And the hostilities are not confined to the great powers of the East and the West. On the contrary, the United States and the Soviet Union, each fully aware of their mutually destructive powers and their world-wide responsibilities and obligations, have on occasion sought to introduce a greater note of caution in their approach to areas of conflict.

Yet lasting peace between East and West would not bring peace to the Family of Man. Within the last month, within the last 4 weeks, the world has witnessed active or threatened hostilities in a dozen or more disputes independent of the struggle between communism and the free world—disputes between Africans and Europeans in Angola, between North African neighbors in the Mahgreb, between two Arab states over Yemen, between India and Pakistan, between Indonesia and Malaysia, Cambodia and Vietnam, Ethiopia and Somalia, and a long list of others.

In each of these cases of conflict, neither party can afford to divert to these needless hostilities the precious resources that their people require. In almost every case, the parties to these disputes have more in common ethnically and ideologically than do the Soviet Union and the United States—yet they often seem less able and less willing to get together and negotiate. In almost every case, their continuing conflict invites outside intervention and threatens world-wide escalation—yet the major powers are hard put to limit events in these areas.

As I said recently at the United Nations, even little wars are dangerous in this nuclear world. The long labor of peace is an undertaking for every nation, large and small, for every member of the Family of Man. "In this effort none of us can remain unaligned. To this goal none can be uncommitted." If the Family of Man cannot achieve greater unity and harmony, the very planet which serves as its home may find its future in peril.

But there are other troubles besetting the human family. Many of its members live in poverty and misery and despair. More than one out of three, according to the FAO, suffers from malnutrition or under-nutrition or both—while more than one in ten live "below the breadline." Two out of every five adults on this planet are, according to UNESCO, illiterate. One out of eight suffers from trachoma or lives in an area where malaria is still a clear and present danger. Ten million—nearly as many men, women and children as inhabit this city and Los Angeles combined—still suffer from leprosy; and countless others suffer from yaws or tuberculosis or intestinal parasites.

For the blessings of life have not been distributed evenly to the Family of Man. Life expectancy in this most fortunate of nations has reached the Biblical 3 score years and 10; but in the less developed nations of Africa, Asia, and Latin America, the overwhelming majority of infants cannot expect to live even 2 score and 5. In those vast continents, more than half of the children of primary school age are not in school. More than half the families live in substandard dwellings. More than half the people live on less than $100 a year. Two out of every three adults are illiterate.

The Family of Man can survive differences of race and religion. Contrary to the assertions of Mr. Khrushchev, it can accept differences of ideology, politics, and economics. But it cannot survive, in the form in which we know it, a nuclear war—and neither can it long endure the growing gulf between the rich and the poor.

The rich must help the poor. The industrialized nations must help the developing nations. And the United States, along with its allies, must do better—not worse—by its foreign aid program, which is now being subjected to such intense debate in the Senate of the United States.

Too often we advance the need of foreign aid only in terms of our economic self-interest. To be sure, foreign aid is in our economic self-interest. It provides more than a half a million jobs for workers in every State. It finances a rising share of our exports and builds new and growing export markets. It generates the purchase of military and civilian equipment by other governments in this country. It makes possible the stationing of $3\frac{1}{2}$ million troops along the Communist periphery at a price one-tenth the cost of maintaining a comparable number of American soldiers. And it helps to stave off the kind of chaos or Communist takeover or Communist attack that would surely demand our critical and costly attention. The Korean conflict alone, forgetting for a moment the thousands of Americans who lost their lives, cost four times as much as our total world-wide aid budget for the current year.

But foreign aid is not advanced only out of American economic self-interest. The gulf between rich and poor which divides the Family of Man is an invitation to agitators, subversives, and aggressors. It encourages the ambition of those who desire to dominate the world, which threatens the peace and freedom of us all.

"Never has there been any question in my mind," President Eisenhower said recently, "as to the necessity of a program of economic and military aid to keep the free nations of the world from being over-run by the Communists. It is that simple."

This is not a partisan matter. For 17 years, through three administrations, this program has been supported by Presidents and leaders of both parties. It is being supported today in the Congress by those in leadership on both sides of the aisle who recognize the urgency of this program in the achievement of peace and freedom. Yet there are still those who are unable or unwilling to accept these simple facts—who find it politically convenient to denounce foreign aid on the one hand, and in the same sentence to denounce the Communist menace. I do not say that there have been no mistakes in aid administration. I do not say that it has purchased for us lasting popularity or servile satellites. I do say that it has substituted strength for weakness all over the globe, encouraging nations struggling to be free to stand on their own two feet. I do say it is one essential instrument in the creation of a better, more peaceful world. And I do not say that merely because others may not bear their share of the burden that it is any excuse for the United States not to meet its responsibility.

To those who say it has been a failure, how can we measure success—by the economic viability of 14 nations in Western Europe, Japan, Spain, Lebanon, where our economic aid, after having completed its task, has ended; by the refusal of a single one of the more than fifty new members of the United Nations to go the Communist route; by the reduction of malaria in India, for example, from 75 million cases to 2,000; by the 18,000 classrooms and 4 million textbooks bringing learning to Latin America under the infant Alliance for Progress?

Nearly two years ago my wife and I visited Bogotá, Colombia, where a vast new Alliance for Progress housing project was just getting under way.

Earlier this year I received a letter from the first resident of this 1200 new home development. "Now," he wrote, "we have dignity and liberty."

Dignity and liberty—these words are the foundation, as they have been since '47, of the mutual security program. For the dignity and liberty of all free men, of a world of diversity where the balance of power is clearly on the side of free nations, is essential to the security of the United States. And to weaken and water down the pending program, to confuse and confine its flexibility with rigid restrictions and rejections, will not only harm our economy, it will hamper our security. It will waste our present investment, and it will, above all, forfeit our obligation to our fellow man, obligations that stem from our wealth and strength, from our devotion to freedom and from our membership in the Family of Man.

I think we can meet those obligations. I think we can afford to fulfill those commitments around the world when 90 percent of them are used to purchase goods and services here in the United States, including, for example, one-third of this Nation's total fertilizer exports, one-fourth of our iron and steel exports around the world, one-third of our locomotive exports. A cut of $1 billion in our total foreign aid program may save $100 million in our balance of payments—but it costs us $900 million in exports.

I think the American people are willing to shoulder this burden. Contrary to repeated warnings, prophecies, and expressions of hope, in the 17 years since the Marshall plan began, I know of no single officeholder who was ever defeated because he supported this program, and the burden is less today than ever before. Despite the fact that this year's AID request is about $1 billion less than the average request of the past 15 years, many Members of Congress today complain that 4 percent of our Federal budget is too much to devote to foreign aid—yet in 1951 that program amounted to nearly 20 percent of our budget—20 percent in 1951, and 4 percent today. They refuse today to vote more than $4 billion to this effort—yet in 1951 when this country was not nearly so well off, the Congress voted $8 billion to the same cause. They are fearful today of the effects of sending to other people seven-tenths of 1 percent of our gross national product—but in 1952 we devoted nearly four times that proportion to this purpose, and concentrated in a very limited area, unlike today when our obligations stretch around the globe.

This Congress has already reduced this year's aid budget $600 million below the amount recommended by the Clay committee. Is this Nation stating it cannot afford to spend an additional $600 million to help the developing nations of the world become strong and free and independent—an amount less than this country's annual outlay for lipstick, face cream, and chewing gum? Are we saying that we cannot help 19 needy neighbors in Latin America do as much for the 19 as the Communist bloc is doing for the Island of Cuba alone?

Some say that they are tiring of this task, or tired of world problems and their complexities, or tired of hearing those who receive our aid disagree with us. But are we tired of living in a free world? Do we expect that world overnight to be like the United States? Are we going to stop now merely because we have not produced complete success?

I do not believe our adversaries are tired and I cannot believe that the United States of America in 1963 is fatigued.

Surely the Americans of the 1960's can do half as well as the Americans of the 1950's. Surely we are not going to throw away our hopes and means for peaceful progress in an outburst of irritation and frustration. I do not want it said of us what T. S. Eliot said of others some years ago: "These were a decent people. Their only monument: the asphalt road and a thousand lost golf balls."

I think we can do better than that.

My fellow Americans, I hope we will be guided by our interests. I hope we will recognize that the struggle is by no means over; that it is essential that we not only maintain our effort, but that we persevere; that we not only endure, in Mr. Faulkner's words, but also prevail. It is essential, in short, that the word go forth from the United States to all who are concerned about the future of the Family of Man; that we are not weary in well-doing. And we shall, I am confident, if we maintain the pace, we shall in due season reap the kind of world we deserve and deserve the kind of world we will have.

Thank you.

[*The President spoke in the Grand Ballroom of the Hilton Hotel in New York City following the presentation to him of the Council's Family of Man Award. His opening words referred to Rev. Dr. Authur L. Kinsolving, rector of St. James Episcopal Church in New York City and president of the Protestant Council, who presented the award; Rev. Dr. Ralph W. Sockman, minister emeritus of Christ Church, Methodist, of New York City, who introduced the special guests; Rev. Dr. Dan Potter, executive director of the Council; Father Kenneth Morgan of the diocese of Brooklyn, cochairman of the Committee of Religious Leaders in the City of New York, who offered the invocation; Rabbi William F. Rosenblum of Temple Israel in New York City, cochairman of the Committee of Religious Leaders in the City of New York, who gave the benediction; Robert F. Wagner, mayor of New York City; Adlai E. Stevenson, U.S. Representative to the United Nations and former governor of Illinois; George Champion, chairman of the board of the Chase Manhattan Bank, who*

★

REMARKS IN NEW YORK CITY
AT THE NATIONAL CONVENTION OF THE
CATHOLIC YOUTH ORGANIZATION
NOVEMBER 15, 1963

Monsignor, Fathers, Sisters, fellow members of the CYO:

I am glad to be here today. I said to the Monsignor coming up that I was pleased to see the Sisters, that in my experience Monsignors and Bishops are all Republicans while Sisters are all Democrats! In any case I am glad to see you and I want to congratulate you on the effort that you are making.

The theme of this meeting is Youth gives Service. And I can't imagine a greater cause in which to be engaged, to give the best that you have, than for the United States. Because on the United States rests not only the burdens of caring for 190 million people but also for hundreds of millions of people around the globe who today without hope look to the United States. Whatever we are able to do in this country, whatever success we are able to make of ourselves, whatever leadership we are able to give, whatever demonstration we can make that a free society can function and move ahead and provide a better life for its people—all those things that we do here have their effect all around the globe.

The world is engaged in the most difficult and trying struggle in its long history. All of the great epics which have torn the world for the last 2,000 years pale in comparison to the great ideological

58

gulf which separates us from those who oppose us. It is our responsibility not merely to denounce our enemies and those who make themselves our enemies but to make this system work, to demonstrate what freedom can do, what those who are committed to freedom and the future can do. So I realize that this meeting is not only a meeting of the youth of today but those of whom we expect so much in the future.

Winston Churchill once said that democracy is the worst form of government except for all the other systems that have been tried. It is the most difficult. It requires more of you—discipline, character, self-restraint, a willingness to serve the public interest as well as our own private interests. All of these Priests and Sisters who have gathered you together from all over the United States don't do it merely because—even though they want you to do well—they don't do it merely because they want four or five thousand boys and girls to do well. It is because they regard you as the future leaders of the United States; as the future leaders of a great free country. That is why I come here today. Not just because you are doing well and because you are outstanding students, but because we expect something of you. And unless in this free country of ours we are able to demonstrate that we are able to make this society work and progress, unless we can hope that from you we are going to get back all the talents which society has helped to develop in you, then, quite obviously, all the hopes of all of us that freedom will not only endure but prevail, of course, will be disappointed.

So we ask the best of you. I hope you will spend your time well now, but I hope that in a long life that you will recognize your obligations to the Great Republic and to help those who need help, to help those millions of boys and girls who drop out of school, who can't find work, who live in underprivileged areas.

I have been impressed by the fact that we have been able to get 10,000 young men and women to go around the world as part of the Peace Corps. But look at all the sections of the United States, in our large cities, in eastern Kentucky, parts of southern Illinois, parts of Ohio, West Virginia, where people live lives of desperation without hope; they look to this country, they look to you, and they look to me to serve. So I hope that all of you will serve—serve not only your families, and your church, but also serve this country. It deserves the best. It has been very generous to us all. And we must be generous in return. So I congratulate you on what you have done, and most of all I congratulate you on what you are going to do.

Thank you.

[*The President spoke at 11:40* A.M. *in the Grand Ballroom of the New York Hilton Hotel to the delegates of the 7th National CYO Convention. His opening word "Monsignor" referred to the Right Reverend Frederick J. Stevenson, National Director of the CYO.*]

2

*PROCLAMATIONS AND
COMMUNIQUES*

* * *

It is fitting that the Inter-Faith Chapel in memory of the American seamen of all faiths who gave their lives at sea be established at Kings Point.

Erected to the Glory of God, this edifice commemorating the memory of these men, will stand as a national monument on the grounds of the United States Merchant Marine Academy where young Americans prepare to serve their country in the American Merchant Marine.

Our Nation has ever sought Divine guidance in its hours of thanksgiving and in its moments of peril.

On the high seas, between heaven and the deep, men of all faiths feel a sense of brotherhood with the infinite.

May this Chapel ever inspire those who pause here to dedicate themselves to the service of their fellow men.

[*The message, addressed to Rear Adm. Gordon McLintock, USMS, Superintendent of the U.S. Merchant. Marine Academy, was read by John S. Stillman, Assistant to the Under Secretary of Commerce.*]

I am happy to extend to millions of our fellow citizens of the Jewish faith, now celebrating Rosh Hashanah, my warm greetings and every good wish for the New Year.

In every celebration of ending and beginning there is both the remembrance of tribulation and the anticipation of good. There is, too, the knowledge that suffering must make both a people and a man more certain of the right, while triumph brings with it the command to respect that right.

This is the hard wisdom of the centuries, marked again with the turning of each new season. We in the United States have found our way as a free people because we have gathered in our own traditions the experience of many peoples and lives. We have learned that tolerance and cooperation are the ways to true national strength. Americans of the Jewish faith have given to their country a great gift in this regard.

I know that all Americans, of every faith, join with me in this greeting and wish for an abundant and peaceful year.

John F. Kennedy

★

PROCLAMATION 3438: THANKSGIVING DAY, 1961
OCTOBER 28, 1961

By the President of the United States of America a Proclamation:

"It is a good thing to give thanks unto the Lord."

More than three centuries ago, the Pilgrims, after a year of hardship and peril, humbly and reverently set aside a special day upon which to give thanks to

God for their preservation and for the good harvest from the virgin soil upon which they had labored. Grave and unknown dangers remained. Yet by their faith and by their toil they had survived the rigors of the harsh New England winter. Hence they paused in their labors to give thanks for the blessings that had been bestowed upon them by Divine Providence.

This year, as the harvest draws near its close and the year approaches its end, awesome perils again remain to be faced. Yet we have, as in the past, ample reason to be thankful for the abundance of our blessings. We are grateful for the blessings of faith and health and strength and for the imperishable spiritual gifts of love and hope. We give thanks, too, for our freedom as a nation; for the strength of our arms and the faith of our friends; for the beliefs and confidence we share; for our determination to stand firmly for what we believe to be right and to resist mightily what we believe to be base; and for the heritage of liberty bequeathed by our ancestors which we are privileged to preserve for our children and our children's children.

It is right that we should be grateful for the plenty amidst which we live; the productivity of our farms, the output of our factories, the skill of our artisans, and the ingenuity of our investors. But in the midst of our thanksgiving, let us not be unmindful of the plight of those in many parts of the world to whom hunger is no stranger and the plight of those millions more who live without the blessings of liberty and freedom. With some we are able to share our material abundance through our Food-for-Peace Program and through our support of the United Nations Freedom-from-Hunger Campaign. To all we can offer the sustenance of hope that we shall not fail in our unceasing efforts to make this a peaceful and prosperous world for all mankind.

Now, therefore, I, John F. Kennedy, President of the United States of America, in consonance with the joint resolution of Congress approved December 26, 1941, which designates the fourth Thursday in November of each year as Thanksgiving Day, do hereby proclaim Thursday, the twenty-third of November of this year, as a day of national thanksgiving.

I urge all citizens to make this Thanksgiving not merely a holiday from their labors, but rather a day of contemplation. I ask the head of each family to recount to his children the story of the first New England Thanksgiving, thus to impress upon future generations the heritage of this nation born in toil, in danger, in purpose, and in the conviction that right and justice and freedom can through man's efforts persevere and come to fruition with the blessing of God.

Let us observe this day with reverence and with prayer that will rekindle in us the will and show us the way not only to preserve our blessings, but also to extend them to the four corners of the earth. Let us by our example, as well as by our material aid, assist all peoples of all nations who are striving to achieve a better life in freedom.

In witness whereof, I have hereunto set my hand and caused the Seal of the United States of America to be affixed.

Done at the City of Washington this twenty-seventh day of October, in the year of our Lord nineteen hundred and sixty-one, and of the independence of the United States of America the one hundred and eighty-sixth.

John F. Kennedy

By the President
DEAN RUSK
Secretary of State.

On the occasion of Rosh Hashanah and the period of the Jewish High Holy Days, I welcome the opportunity to extend to all of our fellow Americans of the Jewish faith my warm greetings and best wishes for the New Year.

In this solemn period you are called upon to rededicate yourselves anew to the faith, the values, the ideals, and the teachings that have stood the stern test of time in your heritage. It is a time for a personal and spiritual inventory and for reflection on goals and achievements. It calls for a reaffirmation of the willingness to sacrifice that there may be righteousness for all mankind.

Never was the desire for genuine understanding among the nations of the world stronger than today. The danger of ultimate disaster increases the urgency and need for a common cause of peace. Our people must lead the way toward relief from oppression, hunger and despair so that all may share in the age-old vision of a good and righteous life.

I know that all Americans join with me in this message of good will.

John F. Kennedy

★

MESSAGE TO POPE JOHN XXIII ON THE OCCASION OF
THE OPENING OF THE SECOND VATICAN COUNCIL.
OCTOBER 5, 1962

Your Holiness:

It is difficult to realize that three years have elapsed since Your Holiness announced that you planned to convene an Ecumenical Council of the

Catholic Church—the first in almost a hundred years. During these three fateful years, millions of my fellow citizens in the United States, including many who do not belong to the Catholic Church, have followed with lively and sympathetic interest the work of the various preparatory commissions appointed by Your Holiness to draw up the agenda for this extraordinarily important Council. They have also read, with particular interest and with genuine admiration for your all-embracing concern for the welfare of humanity, the several inspiring statements issued by Your Holiness on the background and purposes of the Council.

In the face of staggering problems which, from the human point of view, seem at times to be almost insoluble, people all over the world have found reason for renewed confidence and courage in the welcome thought that the Fathers of the Council, as Your Holiness indicated in your Radio Message of September 11, will give special attention to the grave economic and social problems which daily press upon suffering humanity in almost all parts of the world but, more particularly, in the economically underdeveloped nations. It is very heartening to know that the Council, in the words of Your Holiness, will strive to deepen the fellowship and love which are "the natural needs of man" and "are imposed on the Christian as rules for his relationship between man and man, and between people and people."

We hope that the Council will be able to present in clear and persuasive language effective solutions to the many problems confronting all of us and, more specifically, that its decisions will significantly advance the cause of international peace and understanding.

In closing, may I respectfully extend to Your Holiness my warmest personal greetings and best wishes and those of Mrs. Kennedy, who will always cherish the memory of her audience with Your Holiness last March. On the eve of the Council, we earnestly hope and pray that God will continue to bless you with vigorous health and will give you the great joy and satisfaction of seeing the Council fulfill all of your fondest hopes and dreams for a worldwide renewal of fellowship and love and for the establishment of a just and lasting peace.

With sentiments of profound esteem I remain, Respectfully yours,

John F. Kennedy

[*Released October 5, 1962. Dated September 27, 1962.*]

★

PROCLAMATION 3505: THANKSGIVING DAY
NOVEMBER 7, 1962

By the President of the United States of America a Proclamation:

Over three centuries ago in Plymouth, on Massachusetts Bay, the Pilgrims established the custom of gathering together each year to express their gratitude to God for the preservation of their community and for the harvests their labors brought forth in the new land. Joining with their neighbors, they shared together and worshipped together in a common giving of thanks. Thanksgiving Day has ever since been part of the fabric which has united Americans with their past, with each other and with the future of all mankind.

It is fitting that we observe this year our own day of thanksgiving. It is fitting that we give our thanks for the safety of our land, for the fertility of our harvests, for the strength of our liberties, for the health of our people. We do so in no spirit of self-righteousness. We recognize that we are the beneficiaries of the toil and devotion of our fathers and that we can pass their legacy on to our children only by equal toil and equal devotion. We recognize too that we live in a world of peril and change—and in so uncertain a time we are all the more grateful for the indestructible gifts of hope and love, which sustain us in adversity and inspire us to labor unceasingly for a more perfect community within this nation and around the earth.

Now, therefore, I, John Kennedy, President of the United States of America, in accord with the joint resolution of Congress, approved December 26, 1941, which designates the fourth Thursday of November of each year as Thanksgiving Day, do hereby proclaim Thursday, the twenty-second day of November of this year, as a day of national thanksgiving.

I urge that all observe this day with reverence and humility.

Let us renew the spirit of the Pilgrims at the first Thanksgiving, lonely in an inscrutable wilderness, facing the dark unknown with a faith borne of their dedication to God and a fortitude drawn from their sense that all men were brothers.

Let us renew that spirit by offering our thanks for the uncovenanted mercies, beyond our desert or merit, and by resolving to meet the responsibilities placed upon us.

Let us renew that spirit by sharing the abundance of this day with those less fortunate, in our own land and abroad. Let us renew that spirit by seeking always to establish larger communities of brotherhood.

Let us renew that spirit by preparing our souls for the incertitudes ahead—by being always ready to confront crisis with steadfastness and achievement with grace and modesty.

Let us renew that spirit by concerting our energy and our hope with men and women everywhere that the world may move more rapidly toward the time when Thanksgiving may be a day of universal celebration.

Let us renew that spirit by expressing our acceptance of the limitations of human striving and by affirming our duty to strive nonetheless, as Providence may direct us, toward a better world for all mankind.

In witness thereof, I have hereunto set my hand and caused the seal of the United States of America to be affixed.

Done at the City of Washington this 7th day of November, in the year of our Lord nineteen hundred and sixty-two, and of the Independence of the United States of America the one hundred and eighty-seventh.

John F. Kennedy

By the President:
DEAN RUSK
Secretary of State

★

PROCLAMATION 3511: EMANCIPATION PROCLAMATION CENTENNIAL

DECEMBER 28, 1962

By the President of the United States of America a Proclamation:

Whereas January 1, 1963, marks the centennial of the Proclamation in which President Abraham Lincoln declared all persons held as slaves in States or parts of States still in rebellion to be "then, thenceforward, and forever free,"; and

Whereas the issuance of the Emancipation Proclamation marked the beginning of the end of the iniquitous institution of slavery in the United States, and a great stride toward the fulfillment of the principle of the Declaration of Independence that "all men are created equal, that they are endowed by their Creator with certain unalienable Rights, that among these are Life, Liberty and the pursuit of Happiness"; and

Whereas the Emancipation Proclamation and the 13th, 14th and 15th amendments to the Constitution of the United States guaranteed to Negro citizens equal rights with all other citizens of the United States and have made possible great progress toward the enjoyment of these rights; and

Whereas the goal of equal rights for all our citizens is still unreached, and the security of these rights is one of the great unfinished tasks of our democracy;

Now, therefore, I, John Kennedy, President of the United States of America, do hereby proclaim that the Emancipation Proclamation expresses our Nation's policy, founded on justice and morality, and that it is therefore fitting and proper to commemorate the centennial of the historic Emancipation Proclamation throughout the year 1963.

I call upon the Governors of the States, mayors of cities, and other public officials, as well as private persons, organizations, and groups, to observe the centennial by appropriate ceremonies.

I request the United States Commission on Civil Rights to plan and participate in appropriate commemorative activities recognizing the centennial of the issuance of the Emancipation Proclamation; and I also request the Commission on Civil Rights and other Federal agencies to cooperate fully with State and local governments during 1963 in commemorating these events.

I call upon all citizens of the United States and

all officials of the United States and of every State and local government to dedicate themselves to the completion of the task of assuring that every American, regardless of his race, religion, color, or national origin, enjoys all the rights guaranteed by the Constitution and laws of the United States.

In witness thereof, I have hereunto set my hand and caused the Seal of the United States of America to be affixed this 28th day of December in the year of our Lord nineteen hundred and sixty-two and of the Independence of the United States of America the one hundred and eighty-sixth [*sic*].

John F. Kennedy

By the President:
Dean Rusk
Secretary of State.

★

STATEMENT BY THE PRESIDENT ON THE DEATH OF
POPE JOHN XXIII
JUNE 3, 1963

The highest work of any man is to protect and carry on the deepest spiritual heritage of the race. To Pope John was given the almost unique gift of enriching and enlarging that tradition. Armed with the humility and calm which surrounded his earliest days, he brought compassion and an understanding drawn from wide experience to the most divisive problems of a tumultuous age. He was the chosen leader of world Catholicism, but his concern for the human spirit transcended all boundaries of belief or geography. The ennobling precepts of his encyclicals and his actions drew on the accumulated wisdom of an ancient faith for guidance in the most complex and troublesome problems of the modern age. To him the divine spark which unites men would ultimately prove more enduring than the forces which divide. His wisdom, compassion, and kindly strength have bequeathed humanity a new legacy of purpose and courage for the future.

★

PRESIDENTIAL MESSAGE FOR THE JEWISH NEW YEAR
SEPTEMBER 6, 1963

Rosh Hashanah, the start of a new year and the period of the Jewish High Holy Days, affords me a welcome opportunity to extend my felicitations to all Americans of the Jewish faith.

The heritage and religious traditions of Judaism call for a solemn review, at this time, of your deeds and the aspirations of your hearts, so that your lives may be judged and the ennobling goals of your faith reconfirmed. It is also an appropriate time to resolve to take whatever steps may advance the goal of a lasting and universal peace among nations.

We enter the New Year with both renewed hope for a lessening of tensions between people and nations and disappointment in the continuing fires of conflict around the globe. We are committed to the continuing pursuit of liberty and justice, and neither illusion nor disappointments will distract us from our objective. In this basic effort we need the support and commitment of every citizen.

I am sure that all Americans, whatever their faith, join me in extending to each person celebrating Rosh Hashanah best wishes for a happy new year.

John F. Kennedy

By the President of the United States of America a Proclamation:

Over three centuries ago, our forefathers in Virginia and in Massachusetts, far from home in a lonely wilderness, set aside a day of thanksgiving. On the appointed day, they gave reverent thanks for their safety, for the health of their children, for the fertility of their fields, for the love which bound them together and for the faith which united them with their God.

So too when the colonies achieved their independence, our First President in the first year of his first Administration proclaimed November 26, 1789, as "a day of public thanksgiving and prayer to be observed by acknowledging with grateful hearts the many signal favors of Almighty God" and called upon the people of the new republic to "beseech Him to pardon our national and other transgressions . . . to promote the knowledge and practice of true religion and virtue . . . and generally to grant unto all mankind such a degree of temporal prosperity as He alone knows to be best."

And so too, in the midst of America's tragic civil war, President Lincoln proclaimed the last Thursday of November, 1863, as a day to renew our gratitude for America's "fruitful fields," for our "national strength and vigor," and for all our "singular deliverances and blessings."

Much time has passed since the first colonists came to rocky shores and dark forests of an unknown continent, much time since President Washington led a young people into the experience of nationhood, much time since President Lincoln saw the American nation through the ordeal of fraternal war—and in these years our population, our plenty and our power have all grown apace. Today we are a nation of nearly two hundred million souls, stretching from coast to coast, on into the Pacific and north toward the Artic, a nation enjoying the fruits of an ever-expanding agriculture and industry and achieving standards of living unknown in previous history. We give our humble thanks for this.

Yet, as our power has grown, so has our peril. Today we give our thanks, most of all, for the ideals of honor and faith we inherit from our forefathers— for the decency of purpose, steadfastness of resolve and strength of will, for the courage and the humility, which they possessed and which we must seek every day to emulate. As we express our gratitude, we must never forget that the highest appreciation is not to utter words but to live by them.

Let us therefore proclaim our gratitude to Providence for manifold blessings—let us be humbly thankful for inherited ideals—and let us resolve to share those blessings and those ideals with our fellow human beings throughout the world.

Now, therefore, I, John F. Kennedy, President of the United States of America, in consonance with the joint resolution of the Congress approved December 26, 1941, 55 Stat. 862 (5 U.S.C. 87b), designating the fourth Thursday of November in each year as Thanksgiving Day, do hereby proclaim Thursday, November 28, 1963, as a day of national thanksgiving.

On that day let us gather in sanctuaries dedicated to worship and in homes blessed by family affection to express our gratitude for the glorious gifts of God; and let us earnestly and humbly pray that He will continue to guide and sustain us in the great unfinished tasks of achieving peace, justice, and understanding among all men and nations and of ending misery and suffering wherever they exist.

In witness thereof, I have hereunto set my hand

and caused the Seal of the United States of America to be affixed.

Done at the City of Washington this fourth day of November, in the year of our Lord nineteen hundred and sixty-three, and of the Independence of the United States of America the one hundred and eighty-eighth.

John F. Kennedy

By the President:
DEAN RUSK
Secretary of State.

[*Released November 5, 1963. Dated November 4, 1963*]

★　★　★

3

QUESTIONS ANSWERED DURING PRESIDENTIAL NEWS CONFERENCES

* * *

MR. PRESIDENT, your election in November was widely hailed as among other things a victory over religious prejudice. Do you think, as some speculation has already indicated in print, that the seemingly inflexible stand on the part of some spokesmen for the Catholic hierarchy on the school legislation may provoke more religious prejudice?

I AM HOPEFUL that it will not. I stated that it is a fact that in recent years when education bills have been sent to the Congress, we have not had this public major encounter. I don't know why that was but now we do have it.

But everyone is entitled to express their views. The Catholic, Protestant, and Jewish clergy are entitled to take their views. I think it quite appropriate that they should not change their views merely because of the religion of the occupant of the White House. I think that would be unfortunate if they—I think they ought to state what they think. They ought to express their views, they are entitled to do that. Then I will express mine, and the Congress will express its.

I am very hopeful that though there may be a difference of opinion on this matter of Federal aid to education, I am hopeful that when the smoke is cleared there will continue to be harmony among the various religious groups in the country. And I am going to do everything that I can to make sure that that harmony exists because it reaches far beyond the question of education and goes in a very difficult time of the life of our country to an important ingredient of our national strength. So that I am confident that the people who are involved outside the Government, and members of the Congress and the administration, will attempt to conduct the discussion on this sensitive issue in such a way as to maintain the strength of the country and not to divide it.

★

JUNE 27, 1962

MR. PRESIDENT, in the furor over the Supreme Court's decision on prayer in the schools, some members of the Congress have been introducing legislation for constitutional amendments specifically to sanction prayer or religious exercise in the schools. Can you give us your opinion of the decision itself and of these moves of the Congress to circumvent it?

I HAVEN'T SEEN the measures in the Congress and you would have to make a determination of what the language was and what effect it would have on the first amendment. The Supreme Court has made its judgment, and a good many people will obviously disagree with it. Others will agree with it. But I think that it is important for us if we are going to maintain our constitutional principle that we support the Supreme Court decisions even when we may not agree with them.

In addition, we have in this case a very easy remedy and that is to pray ourselves. And I would think that it would be a welcome reminder to every American family that we can pray a good deal more at home, we can attend our churches with a good deal more fidelity, and we can make the true meaning of prayer much more important in the lives of all of our children. That power is very much open to us. And I would hope that as a result of this decision that all American parents will intensify their efforts at home, and the rest of us will support the Constitution and the responsibility of the Supreme Court in interpreting it, which is theirs, and given to them by the Constitution.

★

MARCH 21, 1963

MR. PRESIDENT, are you aware of any international significance to the meeting between Pope John and Mr. Adzhubei, Khrushchev's son-in-law?

NO, SOME HISTORIC interest, but not any underlying international significance. As you know, Mr. Adzhubei stated when he got through that there was no coexistence between the ideologies of Pope John and Mr. Khrushchev, and that has been my view for a long time. But I think that what Pope John is interested in, of course, is seeing—and I think other religious leaders are interested in preventing a nuclear war. So that he believes, I think probably, that communication is one of the means by which we can achieve that objective.

MR. PRESIDENT, how do you feel about the recommendations of the National Academy of Sciences and also of Professor John Rock of Harvard, that the Federal Government should participate actively in an attack on uncontrolled population growth?

WELL, I DON'T KNOW—I am familiar with the general thesis of Professor Rock. As you know, the United States Government today, through the National Institutes of Health, gives assistance to research in the whole area of fertility, biological studies, reproduction, and all the rest, which I think are important studies, and there are several millions of dollars of Federal funds involved, and I think they are very useful and should be continued.

I think the recommendations are that our Government should take the lead and should participate much more actively and strongly than it has done before. You, sir, have never taken a position on this, I believe.

WELL, WHAT IS your question?

The question is: Will you accept the recommendations of the National Academy that we should participate in international birth control studies—provide funds?

WELL, WE ARE participating in the study of fertility and reproduction in the United Nations, which is an international study, at the present time. Now, if your question is: Can we do more, should we know more about the whole reproduction cycle, and should this information be made more available to the world so that everyone can make their own judgment, I would think that it would be a matter which we could certainly support. Whether we are going to support Dr. Rock's proposal, which is somewhat different, is another question.

★

JUNE 24, 1963

MR. PRESIDENT, is there a possibility that you might attend the coronation of Pope Paul VI?

NO, I THINK THE Chief Justice is leading the American delegation to that coronation, although I hope to see him during my visit to Italy.

MR. PRESIDENT, a German newspaper wrote today that, about your next visit to Italy, you are giving more importance as a Catholic to the visit to the Pope than to the meetings with the President, mostly because we (Italy) had a recent crisis and our Government is only a technical one. Could you say anything on that?

NO, I WOULDN'T attempt to comment on that. I am visiting the President of Italy and the Government of Italy. I shall certainly look forward to paying a call on the new Pope. We have a good many matters of concern to us in relations with the Italian Government, not only defense but also economic and trade matters. I think the visit is important. Now, there is never a time when every country in the world is secure and is not having an election. There is no perfect time for visits, I suppose, but I think that this is not an inappropriate time, because I think that 1963 in the summer is the time of change. I would like to see the change be useful and in our favor.

85

MR. PRESIDENT, some Negro leaders are saying that like the Jews persecuted by the Nazis the Negro is entitled to some kind of special dispensation for the pain of second-class citizenship over these many decades and generations. What is your view of that in general, and what is your view in particular on the specific point that they are recommending of job quotas by race?

WELL, I DON'T THINK—I don't think that is the generally held view, at least as I understand it, of the Negro community—that there is some compensation due for the lost years, particularly in the field of education. What I think they would like to see is their children well educated so that they could hold jobs and have their children accepted and have themselves accepted as equal members of the community.

So I don't think that we can undo the past. In fact, the past is going to be with us for a good many years in uneducated men and women who lost their chance for a decent education. We have to do the best we can now. That is what we are trying to do. I don't think quotas are a good idea. I think it is a mistake to begin to assign quotas on the basis of religion, or race, or color, or nationality. I think we'd get into a good deal of trouble.

Our whole view of ourselves is a sort of one society. That has not been true. At least, that is where we are trying to go. I think that we ought not to begin the quota system. On the other hand, I do think that we ought to make an effort to give a fair chance to everyone who is qualified—not through a quota, but just look over our employment rolls, look over our areas where we are hiring people and at least make sure we are giving everyone a fair chance. But not hard and fast quotas. We are too mixed, this society of ours, to begin to divide ourselves on the basis of race or color.

4

EXCERPTS

INAUGURAL ADDRESS
JANUARY 20, 1961

We observe today not a victory of party but a celebration of freedom—symbolizing an end as well as
a beginning—signifying renewal as well as change.
For I have sworn before you and Almighty God the
same solemn oath our forebears prescribed nearly a
century and three quarters ago.

The world is very different now. For man holds
in his mortal hands the power to abolish all forms
of human poverty and all forms of human life. And
yet the same revolutionary beliefs for which our
forebears fought are still at issue around the globe
—the belief that the rights of man come not from
the generosity of the state but from the hands of
God. . . .

Let both sides unite to heed in all corners of the
earth the command of Isaiah—to "undo the heavy
burdens . . . (and) let the oppressed go free."

And if a beach-head of cooperation may push
back the jungle of suspicion, let both sides join in
creating a new endeavor, not a new balance of
power, but a new world of law, where the strong
are just and the weak secure and the peace preserved. . . .

Now the trumpet summons us again—not as a
call to bear arms, though arms we need—not as a
call to battle, though embattled we are—but a call
to bear the burden of a long twilight struggle, year

in and year out, "rejoicing in hope, patient in tribulation"—a struggle against the common enemies of man: tyranny, poverty, disease and war itself. . . .

Finally, whether you are citizens of America or citizens of the world, ask of us here the same high standards of strength and sacrifice we ask of you. With a good conscience our only sure reward, with history the final judge of our deeds, let us go forth to lead the land we love, asking His blessing and His help, but knowing that here on earth God's work must truly be our own.

★

MESSAGE GREETING PRESIDENT QUADROS OF BRAZIL
ON THE OCCASION OF HIS INAUGURATION
JANUARY 31, 1961

. . . . Once in every twenty years presidential inaugurations in your country and mine occur within days of each other. This year of 1961 is signalized by that happy coincidence. At this time, each of us assumes challenging duties for which he has been freely chosen by his fellow citizens. To each of us is entrusted the heavy responsibility of guiding the affairs of a democratic nation founded on Christian ideals and aspiring to common goals of peace and human betterment. . . .

★

REMARKS ON THE OCCASION OF THE CELEBRATION OF
THE CENTENNIAL OF ITALIAN UNIFICATION
MARCH 16, 1961

. . . . The Risorgimento which gave birth to modern Italy, like the American Revolution which led to the birth of our country, was the re-awakening of the most deeply-held ideals of Western civilization: the desire for freedom, for protection of the rights of the individual.

As the Doctor said, the state exists for the protection of those rights, and those rights do not come to us because of the generosity of the state. This concept which originated in Greece and in Italy has been a most important factor in the development of our own country here in the United States.

And it is a source of satisfaction to us that those who built modern Italy received part of their inspiration from our experience here in the United States—as we had earlier received part of our inspiration from an older Italy. For although modern Italy is only a century old, the culture and history of the Italian peninsula stretches back over two millenia. From the banks of the Tiber there rose Western civilization as we know it, a civilization whose traditions and spiritual values give great significance to Western life as we find it in Western Europe and in the Atlantic community.

★

ADDRESS IN NEW YORK CITY BEFORE THE GENERAL ASSEMBLY OF THE UNITED NATIONS SEPTEMBER 25, 1961

. . . . But I come here today to look across this world of threats to a world of peace. In that search we cannot expect any final triumph—for new problems will always arise. We cannot expect that all nations will adopt like systems—for conformity is the jailor of freedom, and the enemy of growth. Nor can we expect to reach our goal by contrivance, by fiat or even by the wishes of all.

But however close we sometimes seem to that dark and final abyss, let no man of peace and freedom despair. For he does not stand alone. If we all can persevere, if we can in every land and office look beyond our own shores and ambitions, then surely the age will dawn in which the strong are just and the weak secure and the peace preserved.

Ladies and gentlemen of this Assembly, the decision is ours. Never have the nations of the world had so much to lose, or so much to gain. Together we shall save our planet, or together we shall perish in its flames. Save it we can—and save it we must— and then we shall earn the eternal thanks of mankind and, as peacemakers, the eternal blessing of God.

★

REMARKS AT BIG CEDAR, OKLAHOMA,
ON THE OPENING OF THE OUACHITA
NATIONAL FOREST ROAD
OCTOBER 29, 1961

I think in these years of great hazard for our country, where we are faced with many challenges, and also I believe many opportunities, that we take our lesson and our theme from the Bible and the story of Nehemias, which tells us that when the children of Israel returned from captivity they determined to rebuild the walls of Jerusalem, in spite of the threats of the enemy. The wall was built and the peace was preserved. But it was written, "Of them that built on the wall . . . with one of his hands he did the work, and with the other he held the sword."

We hold the sword, and we are determined to maintain our strength and our commitments. But we also hold in our hand the trowel. We are determined to build in our own country, so that those who come after us—as they surely will—will find available to them all of the great resources that we now have.

★

. . . . As the Pilgrims gave thanks more than three centuries ago for a bountiful harvest, so we give thanks in 1961 for the blessing of our agriculture and the continued opportunity that the great productivity of our farms gives us in sharing our food with the world's hungry. . . .

. . . . As long as there are hungry families— mothers, fathers, and children—through the world, we cannot possibly believe or feel that our great agricultural production, in any sense, is a burden. It is a great asset, not only for ourselves but for people all over the world; and I think that instead of using the term "surpluses," and regarding it, in a sense, as a failure, we should regard it as one of the great evidences of our country's capacity, and also as a great resource, in order to demonstrate our concern for our fellow man.

As I've said, as long as any of them are hungry tomorrow, I'm sure that Americans will not sit down at their table without hoping that we can do more to aid those who sit at no table.

★

. . . . A year ago, in assuming the tasks of the Presidency, I said that few generations, in all history, had been granted the role of being the great defender of freedom in its hour of maximum danger. This is our good fortune; and I welcome it now as I did a year ago. For it is the fate of this generation—of you in the Congress and of me as President—to live with a struggle we did not start, in a world we did not make. But the pressures of life are not always distributed by choice. And while no nation has ever faced such a challenge, no nation has ever been so ready to seize the burden and the glory of freedom.

And in this high endeavor, may God watch over the United States of America.

★

ADDRESS BEFORE THE UNITED STATES CHAMBER OF COMMERCE ON ITS 50TH ANNIVERSARY
APRIL 30, 1962

For had we achieved these goals of full employment and high capacity, I am confident that none of the events which made this last month so memorable would have taken place at all. And if we can now join in achieving these goals, I am confident that they may never need to take place again.

I realize that we shall not reach these goals overnight, nor shall we achieve them without inconvenience, some disagreement, and some adjustments on every side—among labor, business, and the government.

But the Bible tells us that "there is a time for every purpose under the heaven . . . a time to cast away stones and a time to gather stones together." And ladies and gentlemen, I believe it is time for us all to gather stones together to build this country as it must be built in the coming years.

. . . . When there is a visible enemy to fight in
open combat, the answer is not so difficult. Many
serve, all applaud, and the tide of patriotism runs
high. But when there is a long, slow struggle, with
no immediate visible foe, your choice will seem hard
indeed. And you will recall, I am sure, the lines
found in an old sentry box in Gibraltar:

> God and the soldier all
> 	men adore
> In time of trouble—and
> 	no more,
> For when war is over,
> 	and all things righted,
> God is neglected—and
> 	the old soldier slighted.

★

. . . . The theory of independence is as old as man
himself, and it was not invented in this hall. But it
was in this hall that the theory became a practice;
that the word went out to all, in Thomas Jefferson's
phrase, that "the God who gave us life, gave us
liberty at the same time." And today this Nation—
conceived in revolution, nurtured in liberty, matur-
ing in independence—has no intention of abdicating
its leadership in that worldwide movement for independence to any nation or society committed to
systematic human oppression.
. . . . On this fourth day of July, 1962, we who

are gathered at this same hall, entrusted with the fate and future of our States and Nation, declare now our vow to do our part to lift the weights from the shoulders of all, to join other men and nations in preserving both peace and freedom, and to regard any threat to the peace or freedom of one as a threat to the peace and freedom of all. "And for the support of this Declaration, with a firm reliance on the protection of Divine Providence, we mutually pledge to each other our Lives, our Fortunes and our Sacred Honor."

★

REMARKS AT THE PULASKI DAY PARADE, BUFFALO, NEW YORK
OCTOBER 14, 1962

. . . . Some years ago I visited the Polish cemetery near Cassino, where thousands of Polish soldiers died far from their country in World War II for the independence of their country, and on that cemetery are written these words: "These Polish soldiers, for your freedom and theirs, have given their bodies to the soil of Italy, their hearts to Poland, and their souls to God."

We give our hearts and our bodies to the cause of freedom here in the United States, in Poland, and around all the globe.

★

ANNUAL MESSAGE TO THE CONGRESS ON THE STATE OF THE UNION
JANUARY 14, 1963

. . . . My friends: I close on a note of hope. We are not lulled by the momentary calm of the sea or the somewhat clearer skies above. We know the turbulence that lies below, and the storms that are beyond the horizon this year. But now the winds of change appear to be blowing more strongly than ever, in the world of communism as well as our own. For 175 years we have sailed with those winds at our back, and with the tides of human freedom in our favor. We steer our ship with hope, as Thomas Jefferson said, "leaving Fear astern."

Today we still welcome those winds of change— and we have every reason to believe that our tide is running strong. With thanks to Almighty God for seeing us through a perilous passage, we ask His help anew in guiding the "Good Ship Union."

★

REMARKS IN NEW YORK CITY AT THE DEDICATION OF THE EAST COAST MEMORIAL TO THE MISSING AT SEA
MAY 23, 1963

Admiral Rickover wrote me a few days ago describing the ceremony of the commissioning of a new Polaris submarine, the Andrew Jackson. He said to each captain of a new submarine he gives a plaque which contains an old Breton prayer which was said by fishermen from there for hundreds of years, and the prayer says: "O God, the sea is so great and my boat is so small."

The sea has been a friend or an enemy of us all but it has never, since our earliest beginnings, carried special hazards for the people of this country. We started as a beachhead on this continent; our forebears came by that sea to this land. The sea has been our friend and on occasion our enemy, but to life in the sea with all of its changes and hazards was added the struggle with man, and it is that struggle of nature and man which cost us the lives of 4500 Americans whom we commemorate today.

★

. . . . It is also appropriate that I come to a city which has long been a window to the outside world. As a citizen of Boston, which takes pride in being the oldest city in the United States, I find it sobering to come to Cologne where the Romans marched when the Bostonians were in skins. Many of my educational roots were planted in Boston, but 4 years before Harvard University was founded, this was the city of Albertus Magnus, who taught St. Thomas Aquinas. For Cologne is not only an ancient German city, it is also an ancient European city, a city which, since Roman times, has played a a special role in preserving Western culture, and Western religion, and Western civilization.

★

. . . . Political leaders come and go. What I hope remains between the United States and Germany is not only a strong feeling of sympathy and friendship, but also a recognition in this great struggle in which we now exist, this great struggle to which we have devoted our lives: the struggle to maintain freedom and expand it throughout the world. It is my hope that this country and my own will work in partnership and harmony in the years ahead. That is the best insurance for not only our own survival, not only the peace of the world, but also for the maintenance of that commitment to freedom which I think gives hope of having it spread throughout the globe.

Abraham Lincoln, in the dark days before the Civil War in my own country, said, "I know there is a God. I see a storm coming. If he has a part and a place for me, then I am ready." No one can tell in the future whether there is a storm coming for all of us, but what we can be sure of is that no matter what happens, we believe in God and we are ready.

★

REMARKS IN BERLIN TO THE TRADE UNION CONGRESS OF GERMAN CONSTRUCTION WORKERS
JUNE 26, 1963

I am not a stranger to trade union meetings and therefore I feel most at home here today. I appreciate the invitation which was extended to me through George Meany to join you, Mr. Rosenberg, Mr. Leber, your distinguished Mayor, your distinguished Chancellor, and have an opportunity to talk to those of you whose work is essential in these very difficult and dangerous days.

Below is written a quotation in this building from Benjamin Franklin, which says, "God grant that not only the love of liberty, but a thorough knowledge of the rights of man may pervade all the nations of the earth, so that a philosopher may set his foot anywhere on its surface and say 'This is my country,' " West Berlin is my country.

REMARKS UPON ARRIVAL AT DUBLIN AIRPORT
JUNE 26, 1963

. . . . And then I am glad to be here because this island still fulfills a historic assignment. There are Irishmen buried many thousands of miles from here who went on missions of peace, either as soldiers or as churchmen, who traveled throughout the world, carrying the gospel as so many Irish have done for so many hundreds of years.

So, Mr. President, with the special pride that I feel in my own country, which has been so generous to so many immigrants from so many different countries, I want to say that I am happy to be here tonight.

★

REMARKS ON THE QUAY AT NEW ROSS
JUNE 27, 1963

. . . . I am glad to be here. It took 115 years to make this trip, and 6,000 miles, and three generations. But I am proud to be here and I appreciate the warm welcome you have given to all of us.

When my great grandfather left here to become a cooper in East Boston, he carried nothing with him except two things: a strong religious faith and a strong desire for liberty. I am glad to say that all of his great grandchildren have valued that inheritance.

★

REMARKS AT REDMOND PLACE IN WEXFORD
JUNE 27, 1963

. . . . It seems to me that in these dangerous days when the struggle for freedom is worldwide against an armed doctrine, that Ireland and its experience has one special significance, and that is that the people's fight, which John Boyle O'Reilly said outlived a thousand years, that it was possible for a people over hundreds of years of foreign domination and religious persecution—it was possible for that people to maintain their national identity and their strong faith. And therefore those who may feel that in these difficult times, who may believe that freedom may be on the run, or that some nations may be permanently subjugated and eventually wiped out, would do well to remember Ireland.

★

ADDRESS BEFORE THE IRISH PARLIAMENT IN DUBLIN
JUNE 28, 1963

. . . . In an age when "history moves with the tramp of earthquake feet"—in an age when a handful of men and nations have the power literally to devastate mankind—in an age when the needs of the developing nations are so staggering that even the richest lands often groan with the burden of assistance—in such an age, it may be asked, how can a nation as small as Ireland play much of a role on the world stage?

I would remind those who ask that question, including those in other small countries, of the words of one of the great orators of the English language:

"All the world owes much to the little 'five feet high' nations. The greatest art of the world was the work of little nations. The heroic deeds that thrill humanity through generations were the deeds of little nations fighting for their freedom. And oh, yes, the salvation of mankind came through a little nation."

Ireland has already set an example and a standard for other small nations to follow.

This has never been a rich or powerful country, and yet, since earliest times, its influence on the world has been rich and powerful. No larger nation did more to keep Christianity and Western culture alive in their darkest centuries. No larger nation did more to spark the cause of independence in America, indeed, around the world. And no larger nation has ever provided the world with more literary and artistic genius.

. . . . Ireland is clad in the cause of national and human liberty with peace. To the extent that the peace is disturbed by conflict between the former colonial powers and the new and developing nations, Ireland's role is unique. For every new nation knows that Ireland was the first of the small nations in the 20th century to win its struggle for independence, and that the Irish have traditionally sent their doctors and technicians and soldiers and priests to help other lands to keep their liberty alive.

★

REMARKS AT A CIVIC AND ACADEMIC RECEPTION IN
ST. PATRICK'S HALL, DUBLIN CASTLE
JUNE 28, 1963

. . . . Ireland and education have been synonymous for nearly 2,000 years. For so many hundreds of years this country had colleges and universities of 2,000, 3,000, and 4,000 students in the darkest ages of Europe, which served as the core, as the foundation, for what became the enlightenment and the religious revival of Europe. This country was wise enough to see in days that were past, that when it

finally became independent, that it would need educated men and women.

★

REMARKS AT SHANNON AIRPORT UPON LEAVING FOR
ENGLAND
JUNE 29, 1963

. . . . So Ireland is a very special place. It has fulfilled in the past a very special role. It is in a very
real sense the mother of a great many people, a
great many millions of people, and in a sense a
great many nations. And what gives me the greatest satisfaction and pride, being of Irish descent, is
the realization that even today, this very small island still sends thousands, literally thousands, of its
sons and daughters to the ends of the globe to carry
on an historic task which Ireland assumed 1400 or
1500 years ago.

★

REMARKS AT A DINNER GIVEN IN HIS HONOR BY
PRESIDENT SEGNI
JULY 1, 1963

. . . . Of great importance today, we are trying to
erase for all time the injustices and inequalities of
race and color in order to assure all Americans a
fair chance to fulfill their lives and their opportunity, as Americans, and as equal children of God.
I can neither conceal nor accept the discrimination
now suffered by our Negro citizens in many parts
of the country; and I am determined to obtain both
public and private action to end it.

. . . . One hundred and fifteen years ago this month, Giuseppe Mazzini addressed a mass meeting in Milan with these words:

"We are here . . . to build up the unity of the human family, so that the day may come when it shall represent a single sheepfold with a single shepherd—the spirit of God. . . . Beyond the Alps, beyond the sea, are other peoples now . . . striving by different routes to reach the same goal—improvement, association, and the foundations of an authority that will put an end to world anarchy. . . . United with them—they will unite with you."

Today, Italy is united as a free nation and committed to unity abroad. And beyond the Alps in the capitals of Western Europe, beyond the sea in the capitals of North America, other nations and other peoples are also striving for new association and improvement. By building Western unity, we are ending the sources of discord that have so often produced war in the past—and we are strengthening the ties of solidarity that can deter further wars in the future. In time, therefore, the unity of the West can lead to the unity of East and West, until the human family is truly a "single sheepfold" under God.

★

ADDRESS BEFORE THE 18TH GENERAL ASSEMBLY OF
THE UNITED NATIONS
SEPTEMBER 20, 1963

. . . . Too often a project is undertaken in the excitement of a crisis and then it begins to lose its appeal as the problems drag on and the bills pile up.

But we must have the steadfastness to see every enterprise through.

It is, for example, most important not to jeopardize the extraordinary United Nations gains in the Congo. The nation which sought this organization's help only 3 years ago has now asked the United Nations' presence to remain a little longer. I believe this Assembly should do what is necessary to preserve the gains already made and to protect the new nation in its struggle for progress. Let us complete what we have started. For "No man who puts his hand to the plow and looks back," as the Scriptures tell us, "No man who puts his hand to the plow and looks back is fit for the Kingdom of God."

★

REMARKS AT THE CONVENTION CENTER
IN LAS VEGAS, NEVADA
SEPTEMBER 28, 1963

. . . . There isn't much that you can do today that will materially alter your life in the next 3 or 4 years, in the field of conservation, but you can build for the future. You can build for the seventies, as those who went ahead of us built for us in this great dam and lake that I flew over today. Our task, the task of propelling a third wave of conservation in the United States, following that of Theodore Roosevelt and of Franklin Roosevelt, is to make science the servant of conservation, and to devise new programs of land stewardship that will enable us to preserve this green environment, which means so much to all of us.

And therefore I reach, after 5 days on this trip, three major conclusions:

That we mount a new campaign to preserve our

natural environment in order that those who come after us will find a green and rich country.

Secondly, that we educate our children.

And third, that we use every chance we have to promote the peaceful relations between countries so that we can enjoy what God has given us.

★

. . . . In 1990 the age of space will be entering its second phase, and our hopes in it to preserve the peace, to make sure that in this great new sea, as on earth, the United States is second to none. And that is why I salute Albert Thomas and those Texans whom you sent to Washington in his time and since then, who recognize the needs and the trends today in the sixties so that when some meet here in 1990 they will look back on what we did and say that we made the right and wise decisions. "Your old men shall dream dreams, your young men shall see visions," the Bible tells us, and "where there is no vision, the people perish."

★

. . . . We in this country, in this generation, are— by destiny rather than choice—the watchmen on the walls of world freedom. We ask, therefore, that we may be worthy of our power and responsibility, that we may exercise our strength with wisdom and restraint, and that we may achieve in our time and for all time the ancient vision of "peace on earth, good will toward men." That must always be our goal, and the righteousness of our cause must always underlie our strength. For as was written long ago: "except the Lord keep the city, the watchman waketh but in vain."

APPENDIX

★

★ ★ ★

By the President of the United States of America a
Proclamation:

Whereas the growth of our Nation and the safe-
guarding of its principles of liberty, justice, and opportunity rest upon the Constitution of the United
States; and

Whereas it is most fitting in these crucial times
that all citizens, naturalized and native-born,
pledge themselves anew to preserve, protect, and
defend the Constitution and to rededicate themselves to the service of our country; and

Whereas by a joint resolution approved February
29, 1952 (66 Stat. 9), the Congress designated the
seventeenth day of September of each year as Citizenship Day in commemoration of the signing of
the Constitution on September 17, 1787, and in recognition of those citizens who have come of age and
those who have been naturalized during the year;
and

Whereas by a joint resolution approved August
2, 1956 (70 Stat. 932), the Congress requested the
President to designate the week beginning September 17 of each year as Constitution Week—a time
for the study and observance of the acts and events
which resulted in the formation of the Constitution;
and

Whereas those resolutions of the Congress authorize the President to issue annually a proclamation calling for the observance of Citizenship Day and of Constitution Week;

Now, therefore, I, John F. Kennedy, President of the United States of America, call upon the appropriate officials of the Government to display the flag of the United States on all Government buildings on Citizenship Day, September 17, 1961; and I urge Federal, State, and local officials, as well as all religious, civic, educational, and other organizations, to hold appropriate ceremonies on that day to inspire all our citizens to keep the faith of our Founding Fathers and to carry out the ideals of United States citizenship.

I also designate the period beginning September 17 and ending September 23, 1961, as Constitution Week; and I urge the people of the United States to observe that week with appropriate ceremonies and activities in their schools and churches and in other suitable places to the end that our citizens may achieve a better understanding and a deeper appreciation of the Constitution.

In witness whereof, I have hereunto set my hand and caused the Seal of the United States of America to be affixed.

Done at the City of Washington this fifth day of April in the year of our Lord nineteen hundred and sixty-one, and of the Independence of the United States of America the one hundred and eighty-fifth.

John F. Kennedy

By the President:
DEAN RUSK
Secretary of State.

By the President of the United States of America a
Proclamation:

Whereas the high courage and the supreme sacrifice of Americans who gave their lives in battle have
made it possible for our land to flourish under freedom and justice; and

Whereas the ideals and patriotism of those who
answered the call to service stand as an inspiration
to every new generation of Americans; and

Whereas the same principles and revolutionary
beliefs for which our forebears fought and died are
still at issue in the world and the challenge against
them can be met only through the same qualities of
courage, strength and unflinching determination
shown by our noble dead; and

Whereas Memorial Day each year provides a
fitting occasion upon which our people may not only
commemorate the Nation's heroic dead but also
unite in prayer for the preservation of liberty and
peace free from the threat of war; and

Whereas to this end the Congress, in a joint resolution approved May 11, 1950 (64 Stat. 158), requested the President to issue a proclamation calling
upon the people of the United States to observe each
Memorial Day as a day of prayer for permanent
peace:

Now, therefore, I, John F. Kennedy, President of
the United States, hereby urge the people of the
United States to observe Tuesday, May 30, 1961,
Memorial Day, by invoking the blessing of God on
those who have died in defense of our country, and
by praying for a new world of law where peace and
justice shall prevail and a life of opportunity shall be
assured for all; and I designate the hour beginning

in each locality at eleven o'clock in the morning of that day as the time to unite in such prayer.

In witness thereof, I have hereunto set my hand and caused the Seal of the United States of America to be affixed this 24th day of April, in the year of our Lord nineteen hundred and sixty-one and of the Independence of the United States of America the one hundred and eighty-fifth.

John F. Kennedy

By the President:
DEAN RUSK
Secretary of State.

★

PROCLAMATION 3436: NATIONAL DAY OF PRAYER, 1961
SEPTEMBER 28, 1961

By the President of the United States of America a Proclamation:

Our founding fathers came to these shores trusting in God, and in reliance on His grace. They charted the course of free institutions under a government deriving its power from the consent of the people. In the General Congress assembled they appealed the rectitude of their intentions to the Supreme Judge of the world, and "with firm reliance on the protection of Divine Providence," they mutually pledged their lives, their fortunes, and their most sacred honor.

During the deliberations in the Constitutional Convention, they were called to daily prayer, with the reminder in sacred Scripture it is written that "except the Lord build the house, they labor in vain that build it," and they were warned that without the concurring aid of Providence they would succeed in the political building "no better than the builders of Babel."

In every succeeding generation the people of this country have emulated their fathers in defending their liberties with their fortunes and their lives.

Conscious of our continuing need to bring our actions under the searching light of Divine Judgement, the Congress of the United States by joint resolution approved on the seventeenth day of April, 1952, provided that "The President shall set aside and proclaim a suitable day each year, other than a Sunday, as a National Day of Prayer, on which the people of the United States may turn to God in prayer and meditation at churches, in groups, and as individuals;"

Now, therefore, I, John Fitzgerald Kennedy, President of the United States, do set aside and proclaim Wednesday, the fourth day of October, 1961, as the National Day of Prayer.

Let us all pray, inviting as many as may be visitors in our country to join us in our prayers, each according to his own custom and faith, for our Nation and for all peoples everywhere in the world; and most especially—

For Divine Guidance in our efforts to lead our children in the ways of truth, that they may have the best opportunities we can provide as an environment in which to grow in body, mind and spirit, and to the end that they may be at their best in their day as the responsible trustees of the great heritage which has come to us from those who went before us;

For a spirit of wisdom and understanding, as we move toward new frontiers of cooperation and brotherhood to overcome the curse of hunger, of ignorance, of superstition and of disease, by harnessing scientific knowledge to moral purpose;

For willing hands and a spirit of dedication, that,

in awareness that this Nation under God has achieved its great service to mankind through the toil and sacrifices and subordination of personal desires to common welfare, we may move forward in the unconquerable spirit of a free people, making whatever sacrifices that need to be made to neutralize the evil designs of evil men, and to work for goals of human betterment that lie beyond our span of years;

For peace in our times with freedom and justice and dignity for all mankind; and

Recognizing our own shortcomings may we be granted forgiveness and cleansing, that God shall bless us and be gracious unto us, and cause His face to shine upon us as we stand everyone of us this day in His Presence.

In witness thereof, I have hereunto set my hand and caused the Seal of the United States of America to be affixed this twenty-eighth day of September, in the year of our Lord nineteen hundred and sixty-one and of the Independence of the United States of America the one hundred and eighty-sixth.

John F. Kennedy

By the President:

CHESTER BOWLES
Acting Secretary of State.

★

PROCLAMATION 3442: HUMAN RIGHTS WEEK, 1961
DECEMBER 9, 1961

By the President of the United States of America a Proclamation:

Whereas December 15, 1961, marks the one hundred and seventieth anniversary of the adoption of the first ten amendments to the Constitution of the

United States, which are known as the Bill of Rights; and

Whereas December 10, 1961, marks the thirteenth anniversary of the adoption by the United Nations General Assembly of the Universal Declaration of Human Rights as a common standard of achievement for all nations and all peoples; and

Whereas the Universal Declaration of Human Rights gives fresh voice to the equal dignity and worth of every human being proclaimed in our own Declaration of Independence and in the Constitution of the United States; and

Whereas the strongest guarantee of liberty is the cooperation of independent nations in defense of peace and justice, each in support of its own freedom and the rights of its own citizens:

Now, therefore, I, John F. Kennedy, President of the United States of America, do hereby proclaim the period of December 10 to December 17, 1961, as Human Rights Week, and I call upon the citizens of the United States to honor our heritage by study of these great documents and thereby gain new strength for the long struggle against the forces of terror that threaten the freedoms which give meaning to human existence—the right to speak without fear and to seek the truth regardless of frontiers; the right to worship in accord with conscience and to share the strength and glory of religion with our children; the right to determine our own institutions of government and to vote in secret for the candidate of our choice; the right to justice under law and to protection against arbitrary arrest; the right to labor and to join in efforts to improve conditions of work; the right to unite with our fellows, without distinction as to race, creed, or color, in tearing down the walls of prejudice, ignorance, and poverty wherever they may be, and to build ever firmer the foundations of liberty and equality for all.

In witness whereof, I have hereunto set my hand and caused the Seal of the United States of America to be affixed.

Done at the City of Washington this ninth day of December in the year of our Lord nineteen hundred and sixty-one, and of the Independence of the United States of America the one hundred and eighty-sixth.

John F. Kennedy

By the President:
DEAN RUSK
Secretary of State.

★

PROCLAMATION 3464: CITIZENSHIP DAY AND
CONSTITUTION WEEK, 1962
APRIL 5, 1962

By the President of the United States a Proclamation:

Whereas September 17, 1962, marks the one hundred and seventh-fifth anniversary of the signing of the Constitution of the United States on September 17, 1787; and

Whereas the strength and freedom of our Nation and the fundamental and inalienable rights of our citizens are derived from the Constitution; and

Whereas it is imperative in this time of world uncertainty and unrest that each citizen, naturalized or native-born, be conversant with the acts and events that led to the formulation and adoption of the Constitution in order that he may fully appreciate the meaning and significance of that document and our constitutional form of government; and

Whereas it is fitting and proper on the one hundred and seventy-fifth anniversary of the signing of the Constitution that each citizen renew his pledge to serve his country and to stand ever ready to preserve, protect, and defend the Constitution; and

Whereas by a joint resolution approved February 29, 1952 (66 Stat. 9), the Congress designated the seventeenth day of September of each year as Citizenship Day in commemoration of the signing of the Constitution on September 17, 1787, and in recognition of those citizens who have come of age and those who have been naturalized during the year; and

Whereas by a joint resolution approved August 2, 1956 (70 Stat. 932), the Congress requested the President to designate the week beginning September 17 of each year as Constitution Week—a time for the study and observance of the acts and events which resulted in the formation of the Constitution; and

Whereas these resolutions of the Congress authorize the President to issue annually a proclamation calling for the observance of Citizenship Day and of Constitution Week:

Now, therefore, I, John F. Kennedy, President of the United States of America, call upon the appropriate officials of the Government to display the flag of the United States on all Government buildings on Citizenship Day, September 17, 1962; and I urge Federal, State, and local officials, as well as all religious, civic, educational, and other organizations, to hold appropriate ceremonies on that day to inspire all our citizens to rededicate themselves to the Faith of our Founding Fathers and to the ideals upon which this Nation was established and built.

I also designate the period beginning September 17 and ending September 23, 1962, as Constitution Week; and I urge the people of the United States to observe that week with appropriate ceremonies and activities in their schools and churches and in other suitable places to the end that our citizens may have a better understanding of the Constitution and of the privileges and obligations of United States citizenship.

In witness whereof, I have hereunto set my hand and caused the Seal of the United States of America to be affixed.

Done at the City of Washington this Fifth day of April in the year of our Lord nineteen hundred and sixty-two, and of the Independence of the United States of America the one hundred and eighty-sixth.

John F. Kennedy

By the President:

DEAN RUSK
Secretary of State.

★

PROCLAMATION 3477: PRAYER FOR PEACE,
MEMORIAL DAY, 1962
MAY 18, 1962

By the President of the United States a Proclamation:

Whereas the supreme and selfless sacrifice of those who gave their lives on the field of honor have made it possible for succeeding American generations to remain free and enjoy the spiritual and material blessings of our free society; and

Whereas the courage and ideals of our noble dead have contributed to the advancement of the cause of world freedom and stand as an inspiration to us all; and

Whereas in our time we face a challenge which demands of us the same virtues of loyalty, courage, and devotion to country that characterized our fallen heroes; and

Whereas Memorial Day each year provides a fitting occasion upon which Americans may not only pay tribute to our honored dead but also unite in prayer for success in our search for a just and lasting peace; and

Whereas to this end, Congress, in a joint resolution approved May 11, 1950 (64, Stat. 158), requested the President to issue a proclamation calling upon the people of the United States to observe each Memorial Day as a day of prayer for permanent peace;

Now, therefore, I, John F. Kennedy, President of the United States, hereby urge the people of the United States to observe Wednesday, May 30, 1962, Memorial Day, by invoking the blessing of God on those who have died in defense of our country, and by praying for a new world of law where peace and justice shall prevail and a life of opportunity shall be assured for all; and I designate the hour beginning in each locality at eleven o'clock in the morning of that day as the time to unite in such prayer.

I also urge the press, radio, television, and all other media of information to cooperate in this observance.

In witness thereof, I have hereunto set my hand and caused the Seal of the United States of America to be affixed this Eighteenth day of May, in the year of our Lord nineteen hundred and sixty-two and of the Independence of the United States of America the one hundred and eighty-sixth.

John F. Kennedy

By the President:
DEAN RUSK
Secretary of State.

By the President of the United States a Proclamation:

Whereas faith in Almighty God was a dominant power in the lives of our Founding Fathers; and

Whereas they expressed this faith in prayer, and in this posture members of the Continental Congress mutually pledged their lives, their fortunes, and their sacred honor; and

Whereas each succeeding generation has shared that faith; and

Whereas in full recognition of our dependence upon Almighty God and for our continuing need of His great blessings, the Congress of the United States by a joint resolution approved on the seventeenth day of April, 1952, provided that "The President shall set aside and proclaim a suitable day each year, other than a Sunday, as a National Day of Prayer, on which the people of the United States may turn to God in prayer and meditation at churches, in groups, and as individuals;"

Now, therefore, I, John F. Kennedy, President of the United States, do set aside and proclaim Wednesday, the seventeenth day of October, 1962, as the National Day of Prayer.

On this day, let all pray, each following the practices of his own faith. Let us pray for our Nation and for the other nations of the world. May we especially ask God's blessing upon—

Our homes, that this integral unit of society may nurture our youth and give them the needed faith in God, in our Nation, and in their future;

Our citizens, that they may increase in the desire to promote mercy and justice, peace and freedom, good will and brotherhood, that they may open new frontiers in helping to alleviate hunger, ignorance and disease;

Our Nation, that each new achievement may add to our heritage of faith;

And our world, that this generation may experience the fruits of peace and may know the real meaning of brotherhood under God.

In witness thereof, I have hereunto set my hand and caused the Seal of the United States of America to be affixed this 11th day of October, in the year of our Lord nineteen hundred and sixty-two and of the Independence of the United States of America the one hundred and eighty-seventh.

John F. Kennedy

By the President:

DEAN RUSK
Secretary of State.

★

PROCLAMATION 3536: PRAYER FOR PEACE,
MEMORIAL DAY, 1963
APRIL 26, 1963

By the President of the United States of America a Proclamation:

Whereas Memorial Day provides a fitting occasion for the American people to pause and realize that our Nation has survived recurring crises which have tried the souls of men; and

Whereas we recognize that the maintenance of our freedom has required constant vigilance, unified strength, and the willingness of our people to make all necessary sacrifices; and

Whereas we are accustomed to join together on Memorial Day each year in grateful tribute to our forebears and to our fellow citizens who have given their lives on the field of battle; and

Whereas in memory of their sacrifices in this noble cause we should keep faith with our heroic dead by humbly and devoutly supplicating Almighty God for guidance in our efforts to achieve a peaceful world; and

Whereas to this end the Congress, in a joint resolution approved May 11, 1950 (64 Stat. 158), requested the President to issue a proclamation calling upon the people of the United States to observe each Memorial Day as a day of prayer for permanent peace;

Now, therefore, I, John F. Kennedy, President of the United States, do hereby proclaim Memorial Day, Thursday, May 30, 1963, as a day of prayer for lasting peace, and I urge all citizens on that day to invoke God's blessing on those who have died in defense of our country and to pray for a world of freedom with peace and justice. I designate the hour beginning in each locality at eleven o'clock in the morning of that day as the time to unite in such a prayer.

I also urge the press, radio, television, and all other media of information to cooperate in this observance.

In witness whereof, I have hereunto set my hand and caused the Seal of the United States of America to be affixed.

Done at the City of Washington this twenty-sixth day of April in the year of our Lord nineteen hundred and sixty-three, and of the Independence of the United States of America the one hundred and eighty-seventh.

John F. Kennedy

By the President:
Dean Rusk
Secretary of State.

By the President of the United States of America a
Proclamation:

Our forefathers declared the independence of our
Nation "with a firm reliance on the protection of
Divine Providence." In that reliance, they set forth
the conviction that all men are created equal and
endowed by their Creator with unalienable rights
to life, liberty, and the pursuit of happiness.

More than a century and three-quarters after our
Nation was dedicated to that proposition, it may
truly be reaffirmed that "We are a religious people
whose institutions presuppose a Supreme Being."
Conscious of that religious character of our people,
the Congress of the United States by a joint resolution of April 17, 1952, provided that "The President
shall set aside and proclaim a suitable day each
year, other than a Sunday, as a National Day of
Prayer, on which the people of the United States
may turn to God in prayer and meditation, at
churches, in groups, and as individuals."

Now, therefore, I, John F. Kennedy, President of
the United States of America, do set aside and proclaim Wednesday, the sixteenth day of October
1963, as the National Day of Prayer.

On this day let us acknowledge anew our reliance
upon the divine Providence which guided our
founding fathers. Let each of us, according to his
own custom and his own faith, give thanks to his
Creator for the divine assistance which has nurtured
the noble ideals in which this Nation was conceived.

Most especially, let us humbly acknowledge that
we have not yet succeeded in obtaining for all of
our people the blessings of liberty to which all are
entitled. On this day, in this year, as we concede

these shortcomings, let each of us pray that through our failures we may derive the wisdom, the courage, and the strength to secure for every one of our citizens the full measure of dignity, freedom, and brotherhood for which all men are equally qualified by their common fatherhood under God.

In witness whereof, I have hereunto set my hand and caused the Seal of the United States of America to be affixed.

Done at the City of Washington, this eighth day of October in the year of our Lord nineteen hundred and sixty-three, and of the Independence of the United States of America the one hundred and eighty-eighth.

John F. Kennedy

By the President:

DEAN RUSK
Secretary of State.